Praise for *The "It" Factor*

"Mark Wiskup's latest book, *The 'It' Factor: Be the One People, Like, Listen to, and Remember,* provides an insightful guide on how to build strong connections with our colleagues, family, and friends. Compelling stories, explicit directions, and homework assignments, which allow you to examine your own behaviors in communications, make *The 'It' Factor* a great read for all of us who rely on honest authentic connections in our daily lives."—Dr. Judy Genshaft, President, University of South Florida

"It's career malpractice not to read this book. Mark Wiskup packs more action-ready wisdom about effective communication than you'll find in a hundred books. Run, do not walk, to get *The 'It' Factor*—before your competition does."—Royal Oakes, ABC News Legal Analyst

"*The 'It' Factor* can be the difference between winning and losing . . . Mark Wiskup knows how to make you a winner."—Chip Webster, President, Leadership Centers USA

"Are you climbing the ladder of success and running out of rungs? You need *The 'It' Factor* to reach the top. Mark Wiskup outlines how to make connections with customers, peers, and your boss that others will envy. He even puts together an easy-to-follow plan for you to develop your own 'It' factor. We are committed to Mark's 'It' factor plan and have seen direct results to our bottom line!"—Mark House, Managing Director, The BECK Group

"In this book, Mark Wiskup comes as close as anyone I've seen to the Holy Grail that all learners want: Give me something that will help me, give it to me in plain English so that it's crystal clear, and wrap it in a story so that I'll remember it. *The 'It' Factor* is an enjoyable read that delivers critical lessons for anyone who wants to be a better communicator."—Ed Ruggero, author, *Combat Jump*

"People naturally prefer to do business with people they like. In a world where technology makes us available 24/7 but at the same time leaves us feeling strangely isolated, forming meaningful personal relationships is more important than ever. But connecting with people can be tough, especially for the time-constrained. Mark teaches you how to turn initial encounters into memorable meetings. If your profession

requires you to connect with all kinds of people and personalities, you'll want this book permanently stashed in your briefcase."
—Michelle Bauer, Partner, Sextant Marketing Group

"Working in an industry peppered with jargon and acronyms, *The 'It' Factor* has helped me stand apart from my competitors, and connect with my clients through improved communication skills."—Douglas C. Davidson, Market Executive, Bank of America Commercial Banking

"The 'It' Factor is a no-nonsense, straightforward book useful to professionals at all stages of their career. To have access to Mark Wiskup's insight and wisdom in such an easy-to-read format is phenomenal."
—William F. Sharpe III, Chief Operating Officer, Goldsmith Agio Helms

"The best writers, speakers, artists, teachers, salespeople . . . anyone who is an exceptional communicator exploits *The 'It' Factor*. Mark Wiskup has the uncanny ability to show you how to liberate your 'It' factor. Seize what he says, and you will be the one people like, listen to, and remember."—Ed Dalheim, Founder, MarCom Creative Awards

"Skills that we have learned from *The 'It' Factor* have been invaluable to the whole organization. Mark Wiskup's advice on improving communication has significantly impacted our bottom line. Our salespeople now understand how to effectively sell based on product quality, not price, and have experienced over 30 percent sales growth over a twelve-month period."—Joar Opheim, President, Nordic Naturals

"Smart, practical advice delivered with personality and humor. Reading *The 'It' Factor* is like having your own personal advisor guiding you every step of the way through the potential pitfalls in presenting yourself and your ideas in the most persuasive manner."—Paul Backer, Senior Lecturer, School of Theatre, University of Southern California

"Mark Wiskup doesn't claim to have written a book about sales—but he has! This book won't be found on the sales shelf at your local bookstore—but it should be! *The 'It' Factor* is all about getting others to pay attention to you, to like you, and to find your ideas and requests acceptable, or better yet, desirable. That's the fundamental kernel of sales . . . no matter what it is you sell. I'm telling every salesperson I know to buy this book."—Steve Marx, author, *Close Like the Pros—Replace Worn-Out Tactics with the Powerful Strategy of Interactive Selling*

The "It" Factor

Be the One People Like, Listen to, and Remember

Mark Wiskup

AMACOM

American Management Association
New York • Atlanta • Brussels • Chicago • Mexico City • San Francisco
Shanghai • Tokyo • Toronto • Washington, D.C.

Special discounts on bulk quantities of AMACOM books are
available to corporations, professional associations, and other
organizations. For details, contact Special Sales Department,
AMACOM, a division of American Management Association,
1601 Broadway, New York, NY 10019.
Tel: 212-903-8316. Fax: 212-903-8083.
E-mail: specialsls@amanet.org
Website: www.amacombooks.org/go/specialsales
To view all AMACOM titles go to: www.amacombooks.org

This publication is designed to provide accurate and authoritative
information in regard to the subject matter covered. It is sold with the
understanding that the publisher is not engaged in rendering legal,
accounting, or other professional service. If legal advice or other expert
assistance is required, the services of a competent professional person
should be sought.

Library of Congress Cataloging-in-Publication Data

Wiskup, Mark.
    The "it" factor : be the one people like, listen to, and remember / Mark Wiskup.
        p.   cm.
    Includes bibliographical references and index.
    ISBN-13: 978-0-8144-7437-2
    ISBN-10: 0-8144-7437-3
        1. Interpersonal communication.   2. Business communication.   I. Title.

HM1166.W57   2007
651.7—dc22

                                                        2007001451

Printing number

10   9   8   7   6   5   4   3   2   1

The book is dedicated to Renee, Sharilyn, and Evan Wiskup, who have supported and added insight to my professional passion with more love and concern than any husband or father could ever hope for.

Contents

Acknowledgments

I believe it is always the students who inspire the accomplished teacher, and always the players who drive the successful coach. Therefore, I'd like to acknowledge and thank the participants in my workshops across the U.S. and Canada who make my job a delight, challenge me, and help me to improve my communication skills in every session.

The "It" Factor

The Elusive "It" Factor

PICTURE YOURSELF IN THIS SCENE. You've just stepped off the escalator into the hotel ballroom foyer where your next industry conference will be getting underway in about an hour. You are relaxed and there's a self-assured bounce in your step. As you approach the reception desk, you receive more than a few waves and warm greetings. You recognize someone from last year's meeting, who mouths "I need to talk to you," followed by a quick smile and the raised eyebrows that signal, "I hope you can work me in for a few minutes soon." You return the smile and nod back, letting him know that you want to catch up with him as well.

You feel optimistic. You know this will be a good conference for you, because you have lots to share; at the same time, you also want to hear what everyone else is up to. You can't wait to start the exchange of ideas.

This is what it feels like to possess "It." The "It" factor is the remarkable ability to instantly create honest and powerful connections, in every meeting and every social interaction, every day. It's the seemingly spontaneous skill of making your words meaningful and memorable to everyone, from those who've known you just for two minutes to those who've known you for two decades.

Those who do not have "It" might put down the meeting, calling it a "schmooze-fest," only because they are uncomfortable in this setting. Without "It" they feel isolated and ineffective when it comes to meeting new people and reconnecting with others.

Sure, they'll jump into the mix and start shaking hands, but they don't know what to say or do. They can't connect with others beyond the perfunctory "nice to meet you" and perhaps an obligatory exchange of business cards. Experience has taught them that these efforts will probably be met with a lukewarm reception.

You Can Be the One People Envy

If you've ever felt that others tend to forget what you say, don't listen to what you're saying, or worse, don't take you seriously in the first place, the lessons in this book will change the way you approach every social interaction for the rest of your life.

You will learn how to set an agenda for every conversation, how to use "word pictures" to replace the jargon and overused expressions that sabotage your attempts to connect with others. You'll also see how having "It" will help you succeed, not only in meetings and networking events, but in casual conversations, and even when you have to deliver bad news. You'll feel more poised and confident because you'll know how to handle all manner of interactions, which have been a struggle for you in the past.

Once you know exactly what it takes to quickly build strong connections, you'll start to enjoy tremendous professional and social advantages you never experienced before. Many tasks will come a little easier, and many frustrations will become less intense as, for the first time, others understand what you want and need. You'll also discover you are able to understand what others want and need.

Honest connections translate into dollars-and-cents success. You'll enjoy working with productive and happy colleagues, as well as with trusting, loyal customers who will spend more with your company every year.

Harnessing "It" will also work wonders at home. You will feel welcome relief as you discover your family members are actually listening to your words. They may not agree with you, but they will stop tuning you out!

My goal in this book is to help you become one of those individuals who are admired for being real and genuine in all interactions. As you follow the simple steps outlined in the upcoming chapters you will develop the enviable skill and the advantages that come with possessing "It."

This is not simply "charm" or the ability to always "say the right thing." It cuts much deeper than that. You will learn how to build strong connections, whether you give praise or criticism, both in serious conversations and in light-hearted banter. You will have a rare set of tools that will set you apart from others.

Your new connections will give you personal equity with everyone you meet. Chapter by chapter we will go through the lessons and exercises necessary for you to become a great communicator. You'll learn how to succeed in many situations that up to now you may have approached with apprehension: meetings with your boss, networking functions, or tough conversations with employees who report to you. You'll be pleased to discover there's no mystery to becoming a great communicator, once you have the tools and the desire. By the end of the book, you will have those tools, new confidence, and more success.

You may find some of the lessons perplexing at first, or they may be in direct contrast to other communication chestnuts you've been taught. But contrary to what you may have learned:

- You should not dread delivering bad news.

- Being succinct in your conversations should not be your most important communication goal.

- Delivering a compliment can sometimes do more harm than good.

If some of the tools don't work for you, or don't "feel" right, don't be concerned. You can still be a great communicator by choosing which of these tools to implement. You'll see, just taking the time to consider each tip and incorporating the ones that work for you will make your connections more effective.

In Chapter 11 you'll find a program to show you how to apply all the tools and tips from this book in your personal, professional, and social conversations all day, every day.

Soon you'll have no reason to be jealous of people whose communication you now find awesome. You are about to develop and harness your very own skills. You will be the one others listen to, like, and remember—because you've got the "It" factor.

CHAPTER 1

No One Is Born with the "It" Factor—No Matter *What* Your Parents Say

THOSE WHO HAVE "IT" are just like you, but they have studied, cultivated, and practiced some fundamental skills. They're not more blessed than you are; they're just ahead of you.

"It" takes work and knowledge, not lucky DNA. That means all those people who brilliantly forge instant connections (the people you may be jealous of because you think their people skills come naturally) have deliberately developed their own dynamic "It" factor. Whoa, you say, how can that be? It's not possible. Some people are just too good, too smooth, too charming, and they make it look so easy. They must be naturals!

They aren't. They just know the things you're about to learn about how to connect with others. And they're working at those connections *all the time*. Those men and women you mistakenly pegged as naturals are actually conscious of the steps necessary to become memorable in every conversation and then work those steps constantly.

These powerful, charismatic people, who robustly work a room or a meeting with confidence and apparent ease, are in fact burning lots of mental calories. The great connectors have a specific protocol and mission. They have a clear vision of what they need to do to succeed. And soon you're going to have the vision, protocol, and mission that will help you succeed as well.

Here's the first step in the protocol, the first lesson you must embrace that will lead you to become the one people like, listen to, and remember.

Stop Believing That "Little Voice"

The little voice is very perky, very encouraging, and comfortingly manipulative. The voice talks to you just as you are about to speak to others, and it ruins everything. Here's what the little voice might sound like:

> You know, what you are about to tell them is going to be pretty doggone good. You have something valuable to say, and this will brighten the day of those who hear it. After all, it is coming from you, and your words are precious. People love listening to you, just because you are you!

This voice battles your experience and logic, both of which send up warning flares that this probably isn't true. You've seen far too many slack jaws and glazed-over eyes in the past greeting your words to indicate that the little voice is wrong, and that people probably do not love your words just because they are *your* words.

But, the voice persists. So you wind up still hearing that unendingly encouraging, warm, and compelling voice. It is entirely believable, because it comes from someone you love.

Boring people always give in to that voice. That's why they

continue to be boring with such depressing consistency. The little voice is telling them they are vibrant and compelling, when they are instead dispensing a verbal sedative to everyone in the room.

Every time you put your faith in that little voice, you'll sabotage your attempt to connect with and influence others. Now that you are an adult, you need to learn to put a pillow over that voice and muffle it—constantly. You desperately needed that little voice as a youngster, but it has overstayed its welcome. The little voice is dead wrong.

People will *not* love listening to you, just because you are you. They will love listening to you only after you've built a strong connection with them. It's as simple as this: When you believe that little voice, others will ignore everything you say. That's why you need to tune it out. It's the first step to building strong connections.

Blame Mom and Dad, Then Blame Yourself

That little voice is not really yours. You've *made* it yours, but you are just faithfully repeating what you heard over and over again from the most important people in your young life. It's the voice of your parents that your brain has taken over. (*Disclaimer:* I have done zero homework or research on early childhood development or family dynamics. This hypothesis is the result of my own observations and experience.)

So your journey to becoming a powerful and memorable communicator begins by blaming your parents. Everybody should fault their Mom and Dad. They're the ones responsible for your inability to differentiate between what is tedious and what is compelling when you speak. It's okay. Don't feel guilty for blaming your parents. As an example, let's start with me, and you'll see why I readily blame mine.

That's right, Leon and Doris Wiskup of Manchester, New Hampshire, set me up for failure by stamping an unrealistic set of expectations on my brain about what was supposed to happen every time I opened my mouth to speak. I'm not angry about their parenting and their enthusiastic, never-ending prodding and cajoling of baby Markey to speak, and speak, and speak, and speak. I'm grateful for their indulgence, for indeed I learned to speak and enjoy the sound of my own voice, as we all do.

But all parents (Doris, Leon, and your parents as well!), who energetically hoot and holler with delight every time the little bundle of brains comes up with a new syllable, set in motion a set of deeply ingrained expectations that the outside world will never live up to. The people at work, your customers, your friends—everybody expects way more than your parents did when you open your mouth.

You have to do more than talk . . . you have to *connect*. You have to ignore the little "Mommy and Daddy" voice. Great communicators know the voice is lying, that it takes an effort to show others how good, bright, and talented they are. Connecting is the process of replacing the "Mommy and Daddy" voice with a mature coaching voice that encourages you to build a relationship in every meaningful conversation, instead of just talking to talk.

Let's get back to the parents. I was teasing when I used the word "blame." We should thank them, not blame them, for enabling us to believe all of our words were brilliant. They made the right choice time and time again as they followed their instincts. By jumping up and down the first time a kid sitting in a high chair slurps out "Dada" in between fingering saliva-drenched Cheerios, they helped us. Every parent I know, including myself, greets a child's first few months of talking as if those monosyllabic grunts were more substantive, robust, and inspiring than the Sermon on the Mount, the Gettysburg Address, and the Beatles' first appearance on the *Ed Sullivan Show*, all rolled into one. Their indulgence is critical because babies then learn to like talking, start putting more and more words together, and it all results in more cheers.

So at an early age you are taught by the most important people in your life that just talking and communicating *is* the same thing. And for a while they are. But that only lasts for a year or so. Sadly, even your own Mom and Dad eventually grow weary of your never-ending yapping. After a few years maybe they were bribing you to pipe down for a while so they could watch in peace the antics of that rascal J.R. Ewing and his nutty family on *Dallas*. Devastating, but back in 1981 Mom and Dad chose *Dallas* over you, at least for one hour a week.

This is an early warning signal that few of us heed. This is the moment when we should stop believing that little voice. This is a clear indication, from the creators of the voice (Mom and Dad), that the voice is not to be listened to anymore. The bribe in your hand is the evidence.

As long as you keep listening to the little voice you'll experience isolation and disenfranchisement. Maybe it will happen a little, maybe a lot, but you sure will be frustrated. Remember, it's not that people don't like you; it's just that unlike your Mom and Dad, they don't love you for just being you! And as long as you keep paying attention to the little voice, you're not working the "It" factor protocol. This is the first reason you are not making the impact on others that you want to make.

The Competition to Be Heard Is Intense

When you speak, when you plead, inform, or cajole, you are competing for the attention and consideration of everyone else in the room. It's the *Dallas* scenario played out over and over again. Only no one gives you a bribe to go away. They'll just smile, ignore what you're saying, and easily drift away from you.

And don't fool yourself. They are gone, wondering whether they're getting enough fiber, whether the college bowl games should be replaced by a playoff system, or how in blazes Jack Bauer is going to get out of his current scrape on 24.

The tough thing is you don't know they've left the room, because they're right in front of you, maybe even making eye contact with you as they turn down the volume of your voice and drift away from you to thoughts that are far more interesting. It's depressing: there they are just looking, smiling, maybe even nodding. But, in a cruel twist for you and your happiness, you may not even be close to connecting with them.

They aren't hearing you because they just don't care very much about what you're saying. This may sound harsh, but if you don't accept this, it's going to be difficult for you to muster the energy to do the work necessary to master "It." You have to summon those bitter memories and realize there have been plenty of times when you've been talking and those in front of you haven't heard a word you've said. I say everyone has been and will continue to be ignored.

You and I are "ignorers" as well. As we listen to others, we go through the same exercise of evaluating, staying tuned, or tuning out. This is happening all day, every day. Oh, yes, I do it as well, and I'm not ashamed. Not everyone listens when they probably should, and I say that's a very good thing.

Survival of the species depends on our being able to space out at will when we need to. It's a critical tool that allows us to cope with the gut-wrenching boredom of most conversations, presentations, and meetings, so that open windows and cliffs do not look so inviting. Daydreaming stores our energy and keeps us alive. That's why you have to ignore that little voice and understand that people will drift away at warp speed unless you harness their attention with your words.

So the mission is now clear. You have to be good—not just

accurate, not just right, not just you—to keep them right there with you. It's a competition you want to win so you can build a connection in each and every conversation or meeting. Otherwise, you're making a low percentage bet that *anyone* will listen to you, which is what happens to many of us.

When you ignore that little voice telling you, "Wow, you are really good, just being you," listen to a new voice, one that says:

> "You need to do more than just talk, right now; you have to connect. You need to put some work into this if they are going to care about what you're saying. You may be brilliant, but that's not enough. Start the connection process so they can hear that you're brilliant. If not that, they'll at least hear your words and connect with you."

This competition for the attention of the people in front of you is never-ending. It goes on at every meeting, every conversation, every day of your life, whether or not you want to recognize it. They always have something to think about other than your oration: global warming, tension in the Middle East, or elimination night on *American Idol*.

You may resist the effort and the investment I'm asking for with a shrug of the shoulders and think to yourself, "I'm just not good at that type of thing." But there is significant financial and professional fulfillment you'll be losing every day because of this common, weak cop-out.

Although "just talking" doesn't take much effort, it results in little value and often in mediocrity or even plain misery in the board room, the conference room, and at home. So it's worth the effort to tackle the verbal chores, which those who have "It" take on in every meeting. When you are "just talking" you are listening to that little voice that tells you "just talking" is pretty doggone great. It's not. That's why you have to acknowledge what that little voice has done for you (encouraged you to develop your language skills) and then immediately learn to ignore it. Eventually you'll dump it from your life.

"Just talking" and hoping to make powerful connections is the equivalent of just setting foot in the gym and expecting to become fit and muscular. Even if you're at a top-notch facility, outfitted in some expensive, all-synthetic exercise togs (the ones designed to "wick" off your sweat), you still have to lift the weights, grind it out on the treadmill, or pump your legs in a spinning class to develop the strength, muscle tone, and that endorphin-produced sense of well-being that you want.

It's the same with communication. You've got to put in the work to be a networking and meeting star. When I meet professionals who complain to me they are frustrated by the dolts in their lives who just won't listen to them, I picture a guy walking back to his car after spending ninety minutes doing nothing more than chatting at the gym, lighting up a cigarette, and whining, "I'm just not getting any results from this place!"

He deserves his slothful appearance. And you deserve to be the one whom people *ignore, dislike, and forget* when you don't plan and work to make powerful connections with others. It's tough, I know.

This awakening is what separates the great communicators, the stirring presenters, the successful sales professionals, and the strong leaders from the rest of the flock. But by the time you have "It" you'll know it's a battle for the hearts and minds of everyone you speak to, and you'll be enjoying the battle!

Once you stifle the little voice, you've got big challenges ahead. You are now forced to examine your communication skills with searing objectivity. When the little voice goes away, you may find out you really aren't very effective when it comes to communicating your ideas, thoughts, and dreams. It's not comfy to the psyche, but it's the only way to grab hold of "It," so congratulations.

All strong communicators have reached this point of discomfort. They know that merely speaking fully formed grammatical sentences has nothing to do with communication success. The communication superstars have developed a disciplined routine when they want to deliver their words with power. And they like doing it. It's thrilling and satisfying to connect with others, seeing them perk up and pay attention when you speak.

But that will come later. Right now it's important to understand that there's no way you can create powerful, compelling messages that command respect until you realize that "just talking" isn't nearly enough to succeed.

In Chapter 2 we'll be observing the destructiveness of the little voice in action. You'll meet people who may be just like you. They keep paying attention to the little voice and it keeps them from ever achieving the "It" factor.

Homework Assignment

During the next forty-eight hours, keep track of how many times you zone out while someone else is talking. This is a tough assignment because your brain miraculously allows you to drift away involuntarily (it's that survival instinct!). So if you can recognize your moments of zoning out even just a few times during the next few days, that'll be fine.

When you actually catch yourself tuning out the person who is speaking to you, try to figure out why you are bored. Ask yourself what he should be saying (instead of listening to that little voice inside his head that tells him that he can say anything and people will love it).

And finally, ask yourself the tough question: "If I'm tuning this guy out so easily, without him even knowing it, how many times are other people tuning me out?"

Like all home assignments in the upcoming chapters, you'll have to watch others and then watch yourself to build the skills necessary to have the "It" factor.

CHAPTER 2

The Enormous Value of Building Connections

MY PURPOSE IN THIS CHAPTER is to convince you that striving to build connections is not only a great use of your time and energy, but perhaps the *best* use of your time and energy, starting right now.

In his 1648 treatise, *Leviathan,* philosopher Thomas Hobbes described the misery human beings face when they live outside organized society as "solitary, poor, nasty, brutish, and short." Hundreds of years later I think it's an apt description, at times, of the life of those who cannot create honest connections with others.

You might counter that's "way harsh," arguing that not everyone has to be the life of the party or have a sparkling personality. But I think we can agree that without the ability to quickly connect with others whenever we choose, life can be at times "frustrating, lonely, and unfulfilling" (Wiskup, not Hobbes). There's not much fun—at work *or* at home—when others aren't listening to you, don't give your ideas consideration, don't seek your input, or most painfully, don't seek your company.

You're going to learn this through the case studies of Sheila, Linda, and David. They are the poster children for pursuing the "It" factor.

SHE CAN'T BELIEVE HER EARS

Sheila would be more angry if she weren't quite so stunned. Sitting across from her desk is a defensive and frightened employee named Josh.

"You've gotta believe me, Sheila. I never heard you say you needed the third-quarter financials wrapped up by today," Josh pleads.

Sheila's mind is racing because she knows she can't go to the bank tomorrow without the right financial information. They'll just tell her to come back and apply for the loan when she has her act together. It will ruin her timetable to have to cancel the meeting with the loan officer and embarrassing to show up without her latest financials. Either way, she's stuck in a lousy position. What's even more maddening is that Josh is a strong employee and does a good job for her.

"You mean to tell me you don't remember being in the coffee room last week after we had Chuck's little birthday celebration, when I specifically asked you to get those numbers to me today?" Sheila fumes.

"Well, of course I remember Chuck's party," defends Josh, "But I don't remember you telling me you needed those numbers today."

"Are you looking me in the eye and telling me I never told you that?" demands Sheila.

Josh is convinced he's right and that he hasn't done anything wrong. So he becomes less confrontational than Sheila and not quite so frightened anymore. "Well, you might have said it, but I never heard it. Of course, I know the numbers are important, but I just never heard you say you needed them by today."

Sheila brings the meeting to a close with a grunt and a dismissive wave of her hand. She closes her office door so she can figure out how she got into this mess. She knows she mentioned it to Josh; she remembers the moment exactly. How could he have forgotten, or worse, say he never heard it? How can someone not hear something that is so important to the company and is also a direct and reasonable request from his boss?

In this case, Sheila and Josh are both right. Sheila probably did ask Josh to prepare the third-quarter numbers for her; Josh probably didn't hear it, even though he was sitting right next to her as they were sampling Chuck's birthday cake.

Because Sheila did not connect with Josh, she's going to waste time rearranging her schedule and lose a week or more from her timetable for launching several new programs, which are critical to the success of her business. Sheila was obviously listening to that little voice in her head that we talked about in Chapter 1. There's a lot to lose when you believe the fantasy that people always listen to you, in the real world where people frequently tune you out.

The "Mommy and Daddy" voice told her, "Sheila, your words by themselves are golden. Just tell Josh what to do, and he's got no choice but to do it. You're not only brilliant, you're his boss." So Sheila decided she didn't need to build an instant connection with trusted employee Josh at the office birthday party. Sheila was listening to the "Boss" voice, perhaps, which is a close cousin to the "Mommy and Daddy" voice.

Like the "Mommy and Daddy" voice, the "I'm the boss, damn it" voice is just as dangerous to your success because it reinforces your mistaken supposition that it is neither necessary nor your responsibility to build a connection with others. The "Boss" voice tells you that because someone reports to you they will hear and act upon whatever you request. Every boss knows that in reality this is a hilarious statement, but that doesn't stop the "Boss" voice from luring you into dismissing the need to build connections with everyone. By listening to the "Boss" voice, Sheila winds up being the big loser, and creating a poor leadership example for Josh.

When you can build strong and fast connections with others, you will become a better leader. If Sheila had "It," she would have taken the extra time and exerted the additional energy to be certain she connected with Josh. That would have upped the chances that Josh would "get it" and be motivated to provide her with the financials she needed.

Notice my words, "upped the chances." Those who have "It" know it's not a guarantee for success (after all, there's no guarantee that Josh will come through even if he hears Sheila), just a smart path to bettering your odds. When you have "It" you'll find that not only will you be the one people listen to, like, and remember, you'll also be the one people are drawn to for leadership.

DAVID'S FALL FROM IMAGINED GRACE

As David bounded from the conference room for a quick break, he felt he deserved an icy chocolate coffee drink to celebrate his triumph. The Monday morning meeting had just wrapped up in his company's conference room, and it was a good one for him. Riding down the elevator to the coffee stand in the lobby of the building, he was almost giddy.

Things had not just gone well. It was a total victory for him. Savoring a great start to the week, and enjoying the little buzz he always got from the espresso in the ice-creamy drink, he recounted his superior performance.

David's new plan to boost his company's visibility in the real estate and development community was bold. His firm had always been known as experts in IT outsourcing for the health-care industry. His vision was have the company branch out, attract a whole new customer base, and boost sales quickly; in the process, he would emerge as the superstar. And now, after he had quickly shared his ideas at the close of the weekly meeting and had received a positive response from everyone, he knew he was well on his way.

And the best thing that it took almost no work to get their buy-in, since he had just come up with this plan yesterday. He didn't have it all flushed out yet, but as he laid out his initial ideas and bullet points, he had the feeling he was really on to something. Going in, David knew he would need agreement and support on specific help items from each of the three people in the meeting to put this plan in motion, and he was happy that each of them volunteered to help so quickly. Things start to roll when Susan, his boss and the vice president of sales, agreed to dig through the budget and try to find the dollars for his plan. He needed some seed money to create a buzz in the real estate world and this wouldn't happen without Susan's corporate weight behind the idea. Now that he had her on board, he was rolling. This was a great idea for him and the company!

Denise, his colleague and friend in marketing, was married to a suc-cessful commercial real estate agent, and had promised to ask her hus-band for some critical inside market information and a list of the top players in their region. This would help David to move quickly and elimi-nate months of spending countless hours at meaningless industry net-working functions.

And most importantly, Phil, the research assistant that he and Denise shared, gave a quick thumbs up to doing the homework on the under-served companies in the real estate market. This was the final critical piece to the plan for Dave. He needed to know the exact parameters of the market and where to find the untapped sales dollars that would make this plan a smashing success.

This week was off to a great start, and next week would be even bet-ter. David knew it was childish, but he started imagining what his new embossed cards would look like with the title, vice president of marketing, beneath his name. Boy . . . was he jumping the gun.

It started to unravel quickly. Just after 5:00 P.M. on Wednesday, David poked his head into Susan's office for a quick update.

"How's the mining for dollars coming along, Susan?" David beamed. "Any luck plowing through the budget field and finding our new real estate project funds?"

"Oh, David, I'm glad you asked," Susan said as she looked up from her computer. "Thanks for stopping by. We need to talk about this. After the meeting, I looked at my notes later in the day. I saw you wanted me to look into funding this real estate marketing project you mentioned, but I just couldn't remember a single solid reason why we should invest in it and take valuable dollars away from our current efforts. After all, health care is our core market. So, I'm sorry to disappoint you, but I can't go to bat for you on this one right now. But please work up some more ideas and we can take another look at it, I promise, maybe as soon as next quarter."

David had to call on all his powers of professional concentration to keep from shrieking at the top of his lungs, "Couldn't put your finger on a single *reason*? I gave you some really good reasons. And they were all brilliant! You heard everything I said. I know it, because you were nodding your head. Were we even in the same room, Susan?"

Instead, he kept his cool, and said, "Wow, Susan. I'm surprised, but umm, okay. Thanks for the heads-up. I'll keep working on it and get back to you." He walked back to his office, and tried to clear the ringing in his ears from the blow to the back of the head from this professional two by four.

David is a resilient and optimistic professional, though. The "cup half full" side of him whispered, "Well, thank God I've got Denise and Phil working up their stuff for me. Maybe with the ammo they'll provide me, I'll be able to swing Susan to my side on this, and a lot sooner than next quarter. Though I still can't understand why she didn't get it the first time. Oh well, it doesn't matter. I'm still in good shape with this real estate thing. It will just take a week or two longer, but I'll get there."

David's optimism was misplaced. His second bust in the chops was de-livered on Friday when David and Denise met to discuss the trade show calendar for the following year. As they were wrapping up David thought the time was right to ask Denise what insider's insight her husband Bobby had for them on local real estate players. "Denise, did you have a chance to ask Bobby about which doors we should start knocking on in town to get our new real estate business going? Susan shot down my budget request the other day, and I'm hoping to get some new traction here with Bobby's ideas."

David wasn't prepared for the shock of another disappointment. "Oh, David, I am so sorry. I completely spaced out about this—with everything we had to do for the trade show agenda. Bobby flew to the West Coast this morning for meetings over the weekend, and then next Thursday we're going on that much needed cruise I told you about. But I promise when we get back and settled, I'll make sure I get all the real estate stuff you wanted. I'm sorry, I know I promised it to you, and I meant to talk to him, but I just forgot. Will you forgive me on this one?"

"Of course, Denise, a couple of weeks from now will be fine," David heard himself saying. He had no choice. He was steamed, but he kept it to himself. Denise had been a great support to him, saving his rear end more than once. He respected her and they got along well. And her husband Bobby was a good guy, too. No reason to show a face to her. Plus, she was right, all these trade show details and decisions could be overwhelming. But how could she completely space out about this? She was his marketing department partner, after all, starting at the company at about the same time, sharing lots of successes over the last few years.

David was confused. Denise looked like she was right with him every step of the way as he delivered his dynamite ideas on Monday morning. She not only got a quick handle on the stellar quality of the idea, but readily agreed to lend assistance. Denise was diligent; if she "got" the real estate plan, she'd do everything she could to help, including asking Bobby for some key names. But here it was Friday and she not only came up empty, she said she forgot about it. "Well, I hope Phil doesn't let me down," David said under his breath.

Phil made it a perfect oh-for-three for David on Monday morning. As soon as David saw Phil get out of the elevator, he pounced on him, "Man, please tell me you got that real estate market data you said you'd get for me."

"Hold the phone, Dude," said Phil. David allowed Phil to call him "Dude" even though he was a notch up the company food chain from Phil. There was no harm in it, and David thought it promoted a sense of collegiality in the department. "I agreed to start on it for you. But that's a ton of work. There's no way I could wrap it up in just a week, with all the other stuff you guys handed me."

Very quickly, David was embarrassed to find himself in the middle of a grade school playground beef, which started with, "You did too make a commitment to get that real estate demographic info to me. Come on!"

"NO! I did not agree to that, and you never said you needed it in a week. I would not have agreed to that with everything else Denise and Susan piled on me," Phil responded.

David couldn't keep himself from taking the bait, "I said quite clearly to everyone we needed to roll on this right away. That means I needed your data, and you were in the room, Phil, right next to me when I said it, so don't give me that."

"Ease up, please, David," Phil said, sensing David had lost all patience. "I wouldn't do that to you. I like working with you and Denise, and I'm learning so much here. When you make it clear you're counting on me, I always deliver, don't I? I just flat out did not hear you said you needed that real estate analysis so fast. I hate letting you down. Give me a break on this one."

"Okay Phil, relax. It's okay. We'll go over this later," David said, deciding there was no money in this back and forth with Phil, especially since it was starting to get tense. Phil had made a good argument, and besides, he was dependable and thorough as well. But still, David knew Phil was wrong. He had asked Phil to start compiling the real estate data. He had told Phil how important his role was in the whole initiative. Phil had let David down.

In eight short days, David had gone from dreaming of a vice presidency to wondering if he even had what it took to keep his job here. He thought he had a great idea, and he thought he had everyone's attention. He knew this because there were no naysayers in the room; there was legitimate (if subdued) enthusiasm for his idea to stretch his company's customer base. David wondered how he could have been so wrong.

Everybody was listening to him shine, but nobody really heard him. David believed that because he presented a good idea, even with some accurate assumptions, that Susan would back him. He was wrong; she didn't. David believed that because he made an orderly presentation of his needs that Denise would go out of her way to help him within his time frame. He was wrong; she didn't. David believed that because he was talking about something important, Phil would hear him and push the project to the top of his to-do list. David was wrong; Phil didn't lift a finger to help.

Like Sheila in the first example, David fell victim to the "Mommy and Daddy" voice. And the little voice was tricking him when it whispered, "David, your ideas are so stunning, everyone will love them. You don't need to wait for the right moment, or go to the trouble of showing others the value of this plan. Why, you're *David*, after all . . . just go forward and everyone will cheer!"

They didn't cheer. They may have thought it sounded pretty good for a minute or two, but it wasn't all that memorable. Because David was "just talking" instead of using connection skills, he failed. If David wanted to increase his chances for success (and get those new embossed business cards) he would have developed a strong, instant connection with Phil, Denise, and Susan about the real estate ideas.

David made a common mistake. He thought because he knew and was on good terms with his audience, he could shortcut the hard work part of building connections. There's lots of frustration and heartache in that belief. Sometimes the people you know the best are the ones who are the hardest to connect with when it comes to new ideas. David should have had the patience to wait until he was ready to properly unveil his brilliant idea, because even great ideas are meaningless when you don't launch them with fresh and powerful connections, even with those who know you very well.

Every conversation is a chance for you to connect or to be ignored. You start with a clean slate every time, even with your family, as Linda will find out.

THIS YEAR THE "HELLO DOLLIES" WON'T TASTE RIGHT

There's not a visible square inch of free space on the kitchen counters, as Linda glances at the clock and realizes that her in-laws and cousins are still a good six hours away from walking in the front door. It seems like a long time, but experience tells her that she'll need every minute of those six hours as she pulls the various ingredients for the holiday feast from the refrigerator and meticulously groups them together, by courses.

This "ingredient once-over" step is critical to Linda's holiday feast success. She knows that no matter how detailed the shopping lists are in the last week before the holiday, something always gets missed. It's not a big deal, she's learned, as long as she catches it first thing in the morning. Boy, am I smart, she congratulates herself.

This is what quality control is all about: checking and rechecking. And, it's going to pay off . . . right now. As she pores over the recipe for the "Hello Dollies" that makes her a hit with everyone, every year, she realizes she forgot to buy enough condensed milk. It's the key ingredient to this treat that's been handed down from grandmother, to mother, to Linda.

"Honey, please run to the store and grab two cans of condensed milk for me?" she asks Matt, her husband.

"Um, I can't get out of here for at least an hour or so. I'm still setting up the dining room and the kids table," Matt answers. "It will make more sense for me to stay here and work for a while. I'll be able to get it, along with the bags of ice—in about two hours or so before everyone gets here."

"That's okay, just don't forget," Linda agrees, doing the mental cooking and prep time calculations. "But don't forget. It's very important."

"I won't," he says, and goes about his tasks.

One hour and forty-five minutes before the holiday feast lift-off, he bursts in from the garage. "Wow, are we lucky. These are the last six bags of ice at the store. I'm glad I snapped them up when I did."

"Good job, dear," Linda congratulates him before a wave of irritation crests over her forehead, "but where's the condensed milk?"

"Oh jeez . . . I'm sorry. I forgot," is the pleading and lame reply offered from the next room. "It's just been so hectic all day. And I can't get back to the store now, not with the front walk still a mess. Don't forget, I still have to take a shower and clean up. Can you make do without it? Everything else is going to be great."

"Not really," Linda fumes. "Okay, just forget about it. I'll figure something out. Go do your cleaning."

Linda slams her fist down on the edge of the counter so hard, that the heal of her palm starts to ache. Her brilliant "ingredient quality control" plan has failed. The "Hello Dollies" will miss that magic ingredient that makes them a special delight.

And it's all because Linda's otherwise sweet and thoughtful husband can't follow the simplest of instructions, and remember the easiest of details. "Why didn't he do what I asked? Do I wear a sign that says, 'You can ignore me and my requests, even when you agree to them'?"

Linda pities herself, remembering this isn't the first time she has felt this way. "Why does this keep happening? Nobody listens to me these days."

Linda's suspicions may be accurate. People may *not* be listening to her. But she is misplacing her blame. It's not their fault. It's hers. She's confusing the verbal exercise of talking, even talking about something important (making a holiday meal wonderful for all), with making a connection with and impact on others whose help she needs. Linda won't increase her chances of receiving that help until she learns to build connections by embracing the "It" factor.

Linda believed that just because she said the condensed milk was important, Matt would remember it, amid his jam-packed day. Like Sheila and David before her, Linda wrongly assumed that the importance of the communication means the communication will be heard, remembered, and acted upon. That incorrect assumption will have Linda fretting over the "Hello Dollies" over which she should be proudly beaming.

Sure, it would have taken more time to stop what she was doing and take a few sentences to connect with her husband about the condensed milk, but she thought she didn't have to. She was wrong.

Linda has lots of company. We all repeatedly make the mistake of believing that just because we are talking we are making a connection. It hurts when you talk and others don't listen. It will stop hurting as soon as you realize that talking isn't enough. You've got to work hard at developing and utilizing strong communication skills. You have to build connections with others instead of just announcing information to them.

Sheila's, David's, and Linda's mistakes are ones that we all have committed, at home, at work, at play. We all assume, sometimes frequently, that simply talking is communicating and connecting with others. It's not.

The process of articulating words in your language to others speaking your language does not necessarily guarantee you are making an impact, being persuasive, or being memorable. You may be doing nothing more than making noise, when with a little more effort you could be creating a more satisfying environment for yourself both at home and at work.

We'll return to the travails of Sheila, David, and Linda in the upcoming chapters and see how having "It" would have made a huge difference with those third-quarter financials, the real estate idea, and everyone's favorite dessert.

Observation Assignment

Establish a communication frustration diary. In it I want you to keep track of every instance in which you discover others ignoring or not hearing words, requests, and ideas that you know you have spoken. This will take you a long way toward ignoring the "Mommy and Daddy" voice.

Here's what each entry should include:

• Whom you were talking to

• Where the conversation took place

• What tipped you off to the fact they were tuning you out

• What negative effect this has on whatever process you are currently involved in

You don't have to write down how you "feel" about it. I know how you feel about it. You should "feel" ticked off. What I want you to keep track of is how many times this is happening to you, and how often this lack of connection on your part leads to frustration and wasted energy. This will give you the motivation to tackle and maintain the communication regimen it takes to be the one whom people like, listen to, and remember.

CHAPTER 3

How to Turn Every Conversation into a Connection

OKAY, NOW IT'S TIME TO START THE HEAVY LIFTING. You're ready for it. You have accepted and embraced the news that your words, thoughts, and visions are not automatically creating fits of spontaneous joy in everyone in earshot. You have learned how to ignore the "Mommy and Daddy" voice that has been steering you in the wrong direction.

You also know that to connect with everyone important to you requires a lot more effort than you may have been putting forth, before, during, and after you open your mouth.

Great! Now you are ready to take on the protocol of communication: the orderly steps you have to follow to create powerful connections. This chapter addresses that first step, which is developing an agenda for every conversation.

Let's go back to Sheila, David, and Linda. It's not that they completely destroyed their chances of succeeding by taking the easy way out in each scenario. But they did systematically ratchet-down their percentages of success by following a highly logical but low intensity formula:

- They gave information, which was accurate.

- They asked for help from those who were capable of providing it.

- Their requests were reasonable, and all parties agreed on the action to be taken.

And all Sheila, David, and Linda got for this well-planned, systematic, by-the-numbers communication approach was a healthy dose of frustration. That's because none of them realized they missed the cornerstone of creating powerful, instant connections. They did not make the effort to describe why others should care about what they were saying.

Talk about "Why" Early and Often

Those who have "It" always thoughtfully and energetically explain the purpose of their words. Those who don't do that are lowering their chances and possibly even sabotaging chances of creating connections. The sabotage can always be traced back to the moment when you decided to skip the part where you explain your "why."

Sheila, Linda, and David didn't put enough effort into describing why their requests were worthy of consideration. They quickly mentioned. They hinted. They inferred. They were never compelling. In the end (the beginning too) they thought the reason for their communication was obvious. They were wrong.

Here's how this voice of communication arrogance sounds inside of Sheila's, David's, and Linda's heads: "I said it, and because I said it really well, people should listen." This haughty "why should I go to any more trouble than I have to" attitude toward the communication process and human interaction in general is why Sheila, David, and Linda, and perhaps you, are not receiving the attention and consideration from others that you believe you deserve.

That attention and consideration you crave is like the flow of water. It will naturally follow the easiest course. (I'm guessing here, since I never took physics.) They will pay attention to you, but only if you make it easy for them to do so. Otherwise their attention will flow to something that's easier or more interesting to deal with.

This self-examination is important. It doesn't matter how intrinsically remarkable your ideas and requests are. If you are not humble enough to work to build connections first that will power and guide the positive flow of your ideas, you're in for lots of disappointment.

Great communicators are humble communicators. They know arrogance is the archenemy of powerful connections. And they know that the world is not necessarily a better place just because they are talking. Unlike Sheila, David, and Linda, they understand that merely delivering accurate facts and well-thought-out strategies is rarely ever enough.

Brilliant academics, insightful and creative company presidents, and tireless community leaders can sometimes be crashing bores. We've seen them empty a room just by taking the podium, because they do not have the humility, or perhaps the insight, to recognize that being right, being smart, and having experience is rarely ever enough.

Communication superstars know that they need to do more than just be accurate and right; they first need to convince others that they are worth listening to. Proving they are right might come later. It takes the connection to motivate, inspire, and encourage others.

So, you start building powerful connections only if you can explain exactly *why* you're saying *what* you're saying.

Many scoff at this simple lesson, saying this strategy is overkill and unnecessary work. It's not. It all gets back to humility. When you stay humble, knowing that your words are not naturally brilliant, you will explain your ideas with more energy and passion. This humility will force you to exert the trouble of continually discussing the purpose of what you're trying to accomplish with your words.

You Don't Need the "Why" Every Time

People who have "It" realize they do not have to follow this instruction in every single conversation during the day. They can turn the "Why" explanation on and off when it's appropriate. For example, they know they do not have to tell the server at a restaurant that the reason they are asking for cream is that they like the taste of coffee with cream. It's understood. You don't have to forge an instant connection to get your cream, because it's an automatic, routine request for the server. You're not requiring much effort nor are you imposing on them. Therefore, you don't have to invest much energy in your request.

The same applies to other mundane, low-investment requests, such as:

- Asking to borrow a pen
- Telling the person in front of you in line at the airport that the security guard is waving them over to a newly opened, faster-moving line
- Offering a "Bless You" when someone sneezes

Such momentary exchanges don't merit the effort of explaining your goals and reasons.

When anything more than pedestrian interaction is on the line, however, it's a different story. To increase your chances of success, you should work to go through the paces of explaining why you are saying, what you are saying. This is the best way to start that instant connection process to get others to pay attention to you.

The "Why" Effort Is Efficient

You may immediately protest, "Sorry, brother, no can do. That would just take too much effort, time, and patience. I'm busy, you know." Consider that if your time is at a premium and you are the impatient sort, exerting the effort and extra time to build immediate and strong connections will result in *greater* productivity and success on your part, not less.

Sheila, David, and Linda all took the easy way out and still expected superior communications results.

Sheila was sure when she said to Josh:

> I need those third quarter numbers by next Wednesday, all right?

that it had exactly the same impact as saying:

> Our line of credit comes up for review in a couple of weeks, and the way our business is growing, we're going to need an increase. I've already talked to the bank and they say it won't be an issue, based on our profits, which are way ahead of last year's. All they need to see is the third-quarter Profit and Loss statement when I meet with them on Thursday. Can you have it to me by Wednesday so I can review it before I go into my meeting?

Sheila believes there's no real difference between the more expansive request and the short, glib version she used when she spoke to Josh in between bites of the birthday cake. But after seeing both communications on the same page right next to each other, it's obvious Josh has a lot more reason to tune in to Sheila in the lengthier request than in the shorter one.

When Sheila takes the time and effort to invest in this longer communication with Josh, she's explaining why his work is necessary to help maintain the growth of the company. Had Sheila been more humble in her approach, she could have built an instant, strong connection with Josh. Instead she took her chances with the "I'm the boss" abridged version, with a bad outcome for her and the company. The shortcut was not short after all for Sheila. Now she has more work to do.

David makes the same arrogant mistake as Sheila. That's because he thinks his real estate scheme is an obviously brilliant idea. He believes his remark,

"I think we should look at a new market, like real estate. Can you guys back me up on this? I'm thinking it's really a winner."

is the same as saying:

"This company will increase sales more quickly if we look at growing markets that could use what we sell. I'd like our group to spend some minimal time and money examining this real estate idea. If my gut feeling is right, we can take our current products, and with minor tweaking, sell them to a whole new customer base. It could be a great way to grow our company. I need help from each of you to see if my idea has legs. So, I'm going to make a request. But first, please tell me whether you think I'm headed down the right path with this."

This longer statement requires a lot more energy for David to exert. He thought he didn't have to, that the idea was good enough without all the explanation.

David expects Susan (his boss), Denise (his colleague), and Phil (the research assistant) to give him their time and energy, even when he gave them a minimal amount of his. They said they'd help, and maybe they meant it for a minute or two. But instead, they devoted their energy to competing ideas they found more compelling. They left David's real estate scheme discounted, ignored, and forgotten. Because David didn't take the time to consider this competition for the hearts and minds of his coworkers, he whipped through his request that he thought would help him leap-frog to vice-presidential heights.

The longer presentation might have taken more time, and perhaps it would have been better delivered a week or two later. But spending the extra time would have given David a better shot at success.

To Linda, the sentence:

"Honey, please pick up two cans of condensed milk at the store for me."

is an efficient and entirely acceptable substitute for:

"Everyone will be expecting my "Hello Dollies," especially your Mother. They will all be disappointed if they don't turn out right, and I can see right now that I forgot to get enough condensed milk for the recipe. That condensed milk is the secret ingredient. Without two more cans my favorite recipe is in trouble. Could you please pick them up for me at the store?"

Linda thinks the short sentence did the job of the longer statement, and so should *anybody who knows anything*. Linda will complain that, if she says she needs condensed milk, well then, she needs it, gosh darn it, and 'nuff said for heaven's sake. Does she really have to go to all the trouble of spelling out everything for everybody to get anything done around here? Does she have to explain in detail why she needs help, every time she needs it?

Yes, she does. She must concentrate more on communicating her goals, even to her husband. To increase her chances of success she has to deliver several more thoughtful sentences, and in the process, give up a bit more of her time, which admittedly is at a premium. She thinks she shouldn't have to. Maybe she is right. It just means she's arrogant, unsuccessful, and right all at the same time.

Being right doesn't matter. Don't ever expect others to listen to or follow instructions just because you're right. Being right won't do you any good, unless you first make the effort of helping them care about why you are talking to them.

The people who have "It" know the more you bark orders, the less your chance of building a connection. Great communicators will stay silent when they don't have the time to communicate correctly.

If Linda wants those "Hello Dollies" to garner the familiar praise she's expecting, she has no choice but to slow down and focus on a few sentences of direct communication with her husband. If Sheila wants that bank loan, she has to slow down and explain to Josh why she needs the third-quarter numbers. David needs to stop rushing and explain to Susan, Denise, and Phil why they should spend even a minute on his real estate scheme.

The same goes for you, unless you are:

- A parent screaming at her three-year old to stay in the driveway and keep away from the street

- A judge gaveling for order in the court

- Jack Bauer demanding the schematics from Chloe O'Brien back at CTU so he can save the world from the terrorists.

Screams, orders, and demands always create more problems than solutions in non-life-threatening situations. Bellowing is thus off the table, unless of course you want to create a disconnection.

Humility is the key. When you are humble, you accept that communication success depends on your skills in building a strong connection with the listener. It gets back to that fierce competition for the attention of everyone you talk to. Bosses, husbands, wives, employees, subcontractors, friends—all can and will ignore you at any moment. It does no good to wish and pray they won't.

You don't need divine intervention; all you need to do is start sharing your goals over and over again. As soon as you do that you've automatically increased your odds of keeping them mentally in the room with you.

Sheila, David, and Linda are wasting precious time and valuable energy by keeping their goals under a bushel basket. In their efforts to keeping the communications about the third-quarter numbers, the real estate scheme, and the missing condensed milk short and sweet, they wound up with literally, neither. Bitter, longer, and contentious conversations wound up following what was supposed to be "short and sweet."

Having "It" means you understand the value of pushing your individual communication agendas with more energy earlier in the process, and returning to them throughout. Being a stronger, more powerful communicator, one who spells out goals and reasons quickly, saves time otherwise spent picking up the pieces and sorting things gone awry.

Having "It" Is About Effecting Change

When you harness "It," you're speaking because you want to change the status quo. You want something different from what exists now, and you speak to others in hopes of making that happen.

Every sentence, every conversation, and every discussion we experience is based on this premise. This is an exercise in realizing that <u>when you talk, your goal is to make something new happen, to shake things up—in a big way, a small way, or a medium way</u>.

You may open your mouth because you are advocating a sweeping corporate culture change in your company, or going out for Thai food instead of Italian tonight. Either way your goal is a change in direction.

You may give directions to a lost colleague on the cell phone, or explain to an intern in your office how to fill out a time sheet. Either way your goal is to change their vault of knowledge so they can succeed.

When you tell a joke you want to give them a bit of a chuckle they didn't have before; when you tell a friend disappointing news about the health of a loved one, you want to gain some empathy you sorely need. Either way, you're changing the relationship, ever so slightly.

<u>All talking is about change.</u> That's why those who have "It" don't mind working harder at their communication; in fact they embrace it. They know it's the only way, outside of threatening someone, to have the best chance of getting others to help accomplish change.

Great communicators come to enjoy the challenge of the extra work, beyond just mouthing words. They anticipate the robust competition for the hearts and minds of their listeners because winning and affecting the change in the status quo is very satisfying. Getting what you shoot for always is.

Those who aren't interested in doing the work necessary to build strong, instant connections are not that insightful or diligent. They hate the idea of competing for the hearts and minds of people they are speaking to. They believe they shouldn't have to. They harrumph and fool themselves that the change in the status quo they desire should take place because it is inherently right. Without humility, it's easy to believe others should just "get it," and that they should just respond properly without a lot of fancy explanations.

Those who arrogantly believe that communication should take as little effort as possible face a never-ending series of losing frustrations—at work, at home, and in social situations. The "no-effort" loser communicators tend to become filled with jealousy, often deriding the winners as insincere and manipulative schmoozers.

It's a self-serving stereotype. Gifted communicators may or may not be hiding an evil hidden agenda, just as lousy communicators may or may not be cold and callous. The two are not inherently related.

Let's analyze several scenarios now and see how differently humble winners and arrogant losers approach the same goal and desired change:

Scenario 1: Sales Pep Talk

Scene: Monday morning sales meeting at a computer software firm.

Communication Goal: Tell the team they are behind for the month.

Desired Change: Reverse a negative trend and close sales more rapidly this week.

Winning Communication:

"We're in trouble this month. We're only closing half as many sales as we need to if we are going to hit our goal. If we don't close some sales this week quickly, we are all going to be in hot water with corporate. We need more energy, starting right now."

Losing Communication:

"We're off 48 percent this month. I don't have to tell you what that means. Let's get moving. Now!"

Analysis:

Both speakers were direct and to the point. The winner used more than twice as many words to hit his goal, delivering the bad news in a straightforward, explanatory manner, and he presented a reasonable negative consequence to the team's lack of performance: "We're all going to be in hot water."

The loser was abrupt and delivered a veiled threat. But it all sounded weak, not tough and not inspiring. The words, "I don't have to tell you what that means" were both patronizing and ineffective.

Winning communicators would never use such a phrase unless they were performing in a holiday party skit, mimicking the inane, power-hungry assistant to the assistant manager.

Instead, the winners say directly what they mean without vagueness or resorting to hints. That's the best way to gain everyone's attention.

On the other hand, the losing communicator stands a good chance of being ignored and becoming the subject of rolling eyeballs and disrespectful interoffice e-mails.

Scenario 2: Making a Return

Scene: The cash register kiosk at a trendy upscale boutique.

Communication Goal: To receive store credit for a returned sale item without a receipt, even though it's against the small store's policy.

Desired Change: Trade a poorly fitting item for credit to purchase something that fits.

Winning Communication:

"I need your help. I bought this here last month on sale, without trying it on. This morning I put it on for the first time and was very disappointed to find out it's a full size too small. I have no receipt, which I know is necessary for store credit. Still, I don't want to walk out of here with this useless shirt reminding me of my dumb mistake. Can I get store credit so I can walk out of here, feeling great, with something I'm going to love wearing?"

Losing Communication:

"I bought this on sale last month and it doesn't fit. I don't have a receipt, which I know you usually need to give me store credit, but I'd like you to bend that rule. I shop here all the time and would hate to have to take my business elsewhere if you can't make this happen for me."

Analysis: Both the winner and the loser are clear about their communication goal and what they want. The loser moves straight to a direct, and probably accurate, threat. This tactic, which we all see a lot, is more than saber rattling, because the loser fully intends to storm out of the store, never to return unless he gets that rule bent.

But then he still has a shirt he can't wear, and he has made an enemy. Sure he's macho and to the point, but so what. He still loses. The brevity of those threatening words still adds up to a major waste of time. Threats and coarse behavior are only appropriate when the communicator carefully evaluates the risk of instant disconnects and long-lasting obstinacy on the part of the listener.

The winner, on the other hand, freely admits the mistake was his without undo self-flagellation like, "I am soooo stupid!!!" which would make everyone in the boutique uncomfortable. The winner then spends a few sentences going over the two possible outcomes to the shirt tragedy, neither of which is threatening or manipulative. Discussing a positive outcome is worth the effort for the winning communicator, because he stands a good chance of getting the store credit, and winning a fan in the process.

Scenario 3: Watching Football

Scene: A discussion between a married couple on a Sunday afternoon during football season.

Communication Goal: To have the non-football fan agree to watch the game.

Desired Change: Replace building anger and an impending argument with tranquility and togetherness.

Winning Communication:

"The game comes on in a few minutes, and I want to watch it, start to finish. I know you don't like football, but I know I like hanging out with you. Can I have my cake and eat it too? Will you bring your laptop out here on the couch with me, or maybe just some light reading you need to do? It will make the game more fun for me to have you nearby. The game will be over at four and we can head to Home Depot to get the paint and brushes I know you want."

Losing Communication:

"The game comes on in a few minutes, and I thought even though you dislike football, I'd like you to stay out here. I work hard all week and this is my only chance to veg out. Tell you what: As soon as the game is over, we'll head straight to Home Depot to pick up the paint and brushes you want. I think that's more than fair."

Analysis:

The differences between the two requests are subtle and compelling. Both are reasonable, strong, and accurate. Both describe a fair trade-off. The winner admits the selfishness of the request, with no apologies, and then goes to the effort of describing how he sees the next three hours playing out for his partner. It's strong, direct, and considerate, and it stands a good chance of success with a reasonable partner.

The loser chooses to whine about all the hard work he's put in, and then in the next breath he resorts to playing the fairness card. This all may seem logical to the loser, but it's not a way to win the goal, change behavior, and save time. Instead he succeeds in sounding both boorish and ready for a fight. He's headed for a big-time disconnect with his partner, and perhaps an argument that may bleed into the kickoff. What a disaster!

(For fans of *Dancing with the Stars*, *Grey's Anatomy*, and *The Amazing Race*, just replace the football scenario with your favorite show and promise to hit Home Depot the next day.)

* * * * * *

The lessons of Sheila, David, Linda, and the three scenarios are all the same. Having "It" means that you recognize that getting the benefits of the change you want requires more effort, more time, and more patience than you may think you should have to devote to any meaningful conversation. But that extra work is always worth it because the time, effort, and patience help create far more success and efficiency than quips and brief commands.

Observation Assignment

Make a conscious effort to keep track of how many times you hear meaningful conversations starting with a clear agenda. It's probably fewer than you think, so you should be able to measure how much more interesting you find those conversations. This doesn't necessarily mean that you'll always agree with the speakers, but it does mean you are now listening to them, and that's a win for them.

I'm guessing you won't feel uncomfortable with their directness; in fact, you may find it refreshing and positive. Here are some opening salvos you should look for:

- Here's what I'd like to accomplish with this meeting . . .
- I'd like to start by telling you the purpose of our get-together . . .
- It's important for me to hear what's going on with your project . . .
- I'd like to share a funny story with you . . .
- I'd like to discuss my ideas for a change in our plans . . .

Good luck, and prepare to take on the next phases of harnessing the "It" factor.

CHAPTER 4

How to Build Instant Connections by Painting Pictures with Your Words

I KNOW LOTS OF PEOPLE who travel a lot as a part of their work routine. They love their work, but they also always look forward to returning home after each trip. I am one of those people.

The first thing I want to do after every trip is to spend time with my wife, usually over a relaxing dinner. So as I wait at the gate to board my plane, you would think it might be natural for me to snap open my cell phone, hit the speed dial for my wife, and say:

> **"Hey babe, I miss your face. Let's go out and grab a bite after I land tonight."**

On the surface, these two brief sentences may sound reasonable and mildly affectionate. They are, but they are not connective and would therefore hurt my chances for success at having a dinner date with my wife. It's a low-impact, low-percentage invitation, which in my household would result in the following response:

> "Grab a bite? Well, I don't think so. I'm just not in the mood. There's way too much work around here. What I really want is for you come home and lend a hand."

Any spouse or partner might respond to the "grab a bite" invitation this way because it's a good example of an effortless, mediocre communication. "Grab a bite" is efficient, but worthless because it won't help me to change the status quo. I'm still not going to have that relaxing dinner with my wife. Delivering a fast, efficient, and to the point message means I lose.

"Grab a bite" is too glib and too simple, and it is completely devoid of effort and energy. It's the type of communication that's powered by the "Mommy and Daddy" voice instead of the principles of the "It" factor.

And the negative reaction is exactly what then stuns the lazy communicator, who whines, "Hey, I'm just trying to be nice." This lackluster communicator is talking but not connecting, mouthing brief and pithy words but not doing the real work necessary to build a connection.

The Beauty of the Herb-Crusted Salmon

Let's try again, this time going through the energy necessary to spell out a strong communication action, with a desired change in mind. The key ingredient for communication success is painting a picture:

> "Honey, I've missed you. I want to go out on a special date with you. Instead of going to one of the regular chain restau-

rants near our home, let's go to that little bistro near down-town that you love.

"I know you love the herb-crusted salmon special they offer a couple of times a week. I have the restaurant's number on my cell phone, and I'll call the owner right now and make sure they prepare a portion of your favorite salmon just for you.

"I'll get the pasta con broccoli that's so colorful and fresh. We'll split a big bottle of Italian mineral water. I'll make sure they save a corner window table for us, and place a little votive candle on the tablecloth as a romantic centerpiece for us. After that we'll walk across the street to the coffee house and get a couple of cups of fresh decaf and something sweet and light for us to share. I want us to have a great date tonight. Would you go out with me?"

I have dramatically increased my chances getting the date by taking the time and trouble to paint a picture of what I'll call the "herb-crusted salmon," from now on. The picture of the candles, the mineral water, and the sweet dessert give this communication much more impact than the cool and efficient "grab a bite" request.

It's the picture that will help me connect to her. This specific and calculated communication action will improve the odds of my getting the change I want. I want to go from having no dinner plans to sharing a pleasant evening with my wife.

I know this is not the right picture for every partner. Yours may snicker if you tried it and ask sarcastically what you are up to. Heck, this picture wouldn't work for me if my wife painted it. She'd have better luck suggesting some quick Mexican food and a Quentin Tarrantino Film Festival to build an instant "fun evening" connection with me. But the rightness or wrongness of the "herb-crusted salmon" picture is not what's critical here. When you want to effect a change and alter the status quo, follow the "why" of your communication with a strong visual description of what you want to have happen.

Using the power of painting pictures is the best way to consistently increase your odds of changing the status quo. It's more work, however, no doubt. "Grab a bite" is 17 words, while "herb-crusted salmon" is 177 words. Not only is "herb-crusted salmon" at least ten times as many words, it also takes a lot more thought to put together.

But this is where the payoff comes. When the others in the room sense you are burning a lot of mental calories to connect with them, they will focus more on your words. You are building a connection. They'll find it flattering in a real and positive way. They are now listening to what you have to say, which is what the "It" factor is all about.

"Herb-crusted salmon" allows me to get my wife's attention, forge a connection, while making fast and powerful strides to getting that dinner date. On the other hand, "grab a bite," as efficient and clean as it sounds, hurts more than it helps. Brief communication is rarely powerful communication. It works for giving instructions, orders, or information, but not for building a connection that will create the change in status quo you're looking for.

Pretty Has Nothing to Do with It

Don't let the "herb-crusted salmon" technique give you the wrong impression. When I asked you to always follow the "Why" by painting a picture, I did not use the words "rosy," "pretty," or "pleasing." You may have added those words on your own, believing that taking the trouble to be a communication superstar is merely a saccharin exercise. It's not.

It doesn't matter what your picture conveys—beauty or ugliness, romance or unpleasantness—as long as it fits your communication goal and fosters the change you want to create. Here is an example:

Example: Including a Picture in the Difficult Conversation

Communication Goal: To inform a colleague who reports to you that he is underperforming to the point that he is in jeopardy of losing his position.

Desired Change: To have the junior colleague improve his lagging performance and keep his job.

"Grab a Bite" Communication:

"Your performance is not what we need it to be for you to continue to work here. I hate to do this, but this is an official warning. You have to improve in the next thirty days or I will terminate you. Please pick it up, for both of our sake.

"Herb-Crusted Salmon" Communication:

"Reggie, we are going to have a conversation right now that will not be pleasant for either of us. That's because your performance is not what we need it to be for you to continue to work here. I want you to realize that right now, and I'm hereby giving you an official warning. If you don't improve in the next thirty days, here's what is going to happen. You and I will have a very short discussion, which will include me giving you a severance check and explaining how long your benefits will last. After that you'll start putting all of the pictures of your family in a cardboard box before walking slowly out the door, trying to avoid everyone's pitiful looks and sad good-byes. No one will have much to say to you and everyone will be angry with me. That will be unpleasant for both of us. I'd much rather take you out to lunch in a month to celebrate a great turn-around. But it is up to you to pick up your performance, starting right now."

Analysis: The two communications start the same way. The first one has everything your Human Resources department probably wants you to say, all in just fifty succinct words. It's not cold or harsh. It sounds fair. And it's not nearly as powerful as the second communication.

The "herb-crusted salmon" communication, which consists of 158 words, is much more compelling because of the sad picture it paints, one that anyone would want to avoid. It also convinces Reggie that you really mean it: you will fire him if he doesn't get his act together. Reggie will know this because you have already visualized his termination in your mind, and you can describe exactly how much it will sting.

Harnessing the "It" factor means you are using your valuable energy more efficiently. Painting the "herb-crusted salmon" or "severance check and a cardboard box" picture can save you hours down the road.

Those who have "It" know the goal is not to seek sentences with fewer words, but rather paragraphs with greater impact. They know that this "early impact" of vivid verbal pictures puts the odds of a strong connection in their favor, while saving time and energy later on.

"Herb-crusted salmon" doesn't guarantee that the complaints will necessarily go away, but the consideration and energy devoted to painting a picture of a pleasant evening may reduce the heat of debate and turn it into a reasonable discussion of how challenging it is to keep home fires burning. Both sides will be better off. The additional 160 words will seem like a bargain compared to the thousands of words, perhaps even hostile ones, and hurt feelings you'll both be saving.

The "severance check and a cardboard box" picture could save hours of work and the thousands of dollars that it would take to work with Human Resources, attorneys, and a search firm to get Reggie out the door and find his replacement. And that doesn't even count the lost productivity. Painting a picture is meant to change the status quo and motivate Reggie to start earning his pay. The picture of a dismal firing is the tool that creates a powerful connection, the same way that a picture of a romantic dinner does.

Become an Artist with Your Words

It's not hard or intellectually challenging to paint a picture with your words. It just takes the ability to put a pillow over the "Mommy and Daddy" voice, as well as ending the drive for efficiency with your words. You'll want to paint pictures when you realize it's the path to success and actually saves you work in the long run.

Let's take a cue from our examples to learn how to develop quick and powerful pictures with your words.

Be direct in the first sentence or two to get your communication goal right out front. It makes your agenda and desire for change in the status quo clear. With this opening you stand a good chance of grabbing the attention of the listener. That means they'll be ready for the picture you're about to paint. A direct, straightforward sentence or two is also a good way to prompt you to paint a picture. It's also extremely considerate, but we'll get to that in a page or two.

Let's go back to the opening sentences of our successful picture-painting examples:

> "Honey, I've missed you. I want to go out on a special date with you."

This wording creates greater impact than the more mundane:

"Maybe we should take a minute or two to discuss some dinner plans."

As for the "difficult conversation" example, I don't find that walking softly on the way to deliver bad news is helpful. Strong and direct can also be kind and thoughtful:

"Reggie, we are going to have a conversation right now that will not be pleasant for either of us. That's because your performance is not what we need it to be for you to continue to work here."

This wording creates greater impact than the more feeble:

"We all know it's important to constantly evaluate all of our individual performances in regard to our corporate goals, so I wanted to take a few minutes to talk with you."

There's nothing wrong with weaker, softer approaches. They're inoffensive. They are okay. But "okay" is a losing proposition when your goal is to create an immediate impact and effect change. "Okay" is for those who are *not* interested in the benefits of the "It" factor. So your goal must be to do *better* than "okay." And better starts with a powerful, incisive sentence or two.

This directness in tone and approach may create a sense of discomfort for you. I understand that, and lots of my clients say the same thing. So consider that directness, kindness, and empathy all work together very nicely. It is the direct statement of a communication goal that shows the height of consideration.

By being direct and at the same time considerate, you are treating the people you are addressing with respect. Your directness shows you are not patronizing them by attempting to soften the blow or easing them into understanding your key communication goal. Speaking directly stops you from delivering the disconnecting message, "Oh, fragile little thing, I must be gentle," or "Oh, I'm going to slow this whole discussion down a bit, so even someone like you can grasp it."

Because you respect them and their integrity, you show right away where you are going with your messages, positive or negative. Don't think of the word "direct" as meaning abrupt, harsh, or cold. A direct opening sentence, one that sets the scene for a powerful word picture, can also be thoughtful and reasonable, as long as it's well conceived and followed by the simplest of communication tools: a pause.

A Breath Is a Delight and a Great Tool

Poor communicators tend to rush through their words and messages, just eager for the conversation or the meeting to conclude so they don't have to be on the spot. The best communicators pause frequently and enjoy the impact of their message. When these pros are at the top of their game, they follow each direct communication goal statement with a healthy pause—before they go on to painting their picture. Their audience may not yet be agreeing, but they surely *are* listening. All because of that beat of silence.

That brief pause draws everyone in the room closer, creating a moment of elegant drama and setting the proper tone for the picture you are about to paint. The pause—the silent beat—is a brilliant little tool to focus the attention of your listeners on your key messages. When you start pausing to draw others closer to your words and ideas, you will be in great company. From Marlon Brando's chastising of Rod Steiger during the "I coulda been a contender" speech in *On the Waterfront*, to Robert De Niro's chilling "You talkin' to me" mayhem rehearsal in *Taxi Driver,* to Beethoven's Fifth Symphony, to the Rolling Stones' opening chords of "Start Me Up"—the silent dramatic beat between phrases creates the power of these performances. Develop the discipline to pause, and you will compel every listener to focus on your words. It will give the word pictures that follow the attention they deserve.

The first few times you force yourself to pause for that compelling beat, you may feel uncomfortable. You may worry that others in the room may think you are not sure where you are headed, or that you will be criticized for being overly dramatic or manipulative. Dismiss these concerns.

My coaching experiences tell me when you are starting to feel uneasy with your pause, you're pausing just the perfect amount of time to create that drama and power that will help you. Just be sure that when you pause, you are well aware of what you're going to say next. Your communications goal at that moment is sincere. You want to bring focus and power to your words. The audience will be there with you, eagerly waiting for your next words.

Painting a Picture Is Easy: Just Put Us There

Now we're getting to the technical construction of your word pictures. It's easier than you think, and it doesn't require creativity or artistic talent. All it takes is the ability to follow the *rule of three objects and three actions.*

Here's the rule in brief: *Your direct opening sentences will take on a new vibrancy and meaning when you follow them with your description of a scene that involves three objects and three actions.*

That's the math. Don't go nuts on Google trying to find my source on this. You won't find any reference to it. It's my rule. I made it up. And it works. Here is a specific example of how the rule of three objects and three actions make your words come alive and get your audience listening to you.

Example: New Software Application

Here is a communication prior to applying the rule of three:

> "You'll love the new software application. It's going to be great for our department."

There's nothing wrong with these sentences, but there's nothing right with them either. That means you can't count on making much of a connection. Let's add the rule of three and make it work much better:

> "You'll love the new software application. It's going to be great for us. When I tested (action #1) the demo last week on Steve's computer (object #1) I couldn't believe how quickly I was flying (action #2) between each of our customer data bases, one after another popping up (action #3) on the screen (object #2). The data was coming up as soon as I touched the track wheel (object #3) on the mouse."

The second picture illustrates how cool the new software is, and how it will make the team more productive. (Note that I did not count the nonvisual nouns—customer data bases, data—as objects, and that the "mouse" could count as a fourth object.)

The best use of the rule of three is to fight to get three real objects—objects that someone can visualize—into your picture, and then put them into the middle of three distinct actions. Up to this point in the book I've been mentioning all the extra work and energy that is needed to build powerful connections. *This then is the work:* painting the pictures with at least three objects and three actions, every time you want to be heard.

This is your decision point. This is the epicenter of powerful communication. And this is the extra work that you'll spend again and again when you get "It."

Although it takes constant effort to apply the rule of three for all of your conversations and presentations, it requires no financial or physical sacrifice. It's really a bargain! You give up so little and you get so much in return. Let's take a look at how painting a picture using the rule of three works in the "herb-crusted salmon" and the "difficult conversation" examples.

Example: Herb-Crusted Salmon

"Honey, I've missed you. I want to go (action #1) out on a special date with you. Instead of going (action #2) to one of the regular chain restaurants (object#1) near our home (object #2), let's go (action #3) to that little bistro (object #3) near downtown (object #4) that you love.

"I know you love the herb-crusted salmon special (object #5) they offer a couple of times a week. I have the restaurant's number (object #6) on my cell phone (object #7) and I'll call (action #4) the owner (object #8) right now and make sure they prepare (action #5) a portion of your favorite salmon (object #9) just for you.

"I'll order (action #6) the pasta con broccoli (object #10) that's so colorful and fresh. We'll split (action #7) a big bottle of Italian mineral water (object #11). I'll make sure they save (action #8) a corner window table (object #12) for us, and place (action #9) a little votive candle (object #13) on the tablecloth (object #14) as a romantic centerpiece (object #15) for us. After that we'll stroll (action #10) across the street (object #16) to the coffee house (object #17) and order (action #11) a couple of cups of fresh decaf (object #18) and something sweet and light (object #19) for us to share (action #12). I want us to have a great date tonight. Could you go (action #13) out with me (object #20)?"

The "herb-crusted salmon" picture, which has twenty objects and thirteen actions, paints a powerful picture for my wife to consider because it contains all the things she likes in an evening out. It also takes a lot of work and thought for me to deliver it.

That's important. If you want to win them over, or at least get their attention, the best way to do it is to show that you are willing to invest in the conversation. Every time you paint a picture you are demonstrating your commitment to the conversation. You are proving to the listener that you care about connecting with them. It's difficult for anyone to ignore someone who demonstrates humility and hard work, all at the same time.

The "grab a bite" communication, on the other hand, has one action and one object. Not much thought, just a punchy request with little investment. When you don't invest in painting pictures for your listeners, don't expect much of a connection. When you don't show you care, they won't either.

- Example: Difficult Conversation

Let's conduct the same analysis on the difficult conversation with Reggie. Notice the object/action words don't kick in for a sentence or two:

"Reggie, we are going to have a conversation right now that will not be pleasant for either of us. That's because your per-formance is not what we need it to be for you to continue to work here. I want you to realize that right now, and I'm hereby giving you an official warning. If you don't improve in the next thirty days, here's what going to happen.

"You and I will have a very short discussion, which will include me giving you (action #1) a severance check (object #1) and explaining (action #2) how long your benefits will last. After that you'll start putting (action #3) all of the pictures (object #2), of your family in a cardboard box (object #3) before walking slowly (action #4) out the door (object #4), trying to avoid (action #5) everyone's pitiful looks (object #5) and sad good-byes. That will be unpleasant for both of us. Pick up (action #6) your performance, right now, so I can take you out (action #7) for a steak dinner (object #6) in a month to celebrate (action #8) a great turn-around."

This dramatic little picture of a firing contains eight different actions and six different objects. The picture is accurate, too, as those of us who have been on either end of a conversation like this fully understand. Here again I counted just the actions and objects, not all the verbs and nouns. You need the real objects and action verbs to create a picture, instead of just an accurate communication.

All these well-laid-out objects and actions are designed to show Reggie that this is a serious and real warning, and they should dispel any notions Reggie may have that the boss may just be having a bad day and doesn't really mean it. It also should foster a stronger connection between Reggie and his boss. When the boss takes the trouble to put together a picture that includes eight different actions and six objects it shows Reggie a tremendous amount of respect and concern. It's a tough message. But because the boss put so much effort into it, it is a message that will connect with Reggie and give him a harsh but necessary wake-up call.

Painting a Picture Gives You Executive Presence

Friends and colleagues frequently tell me they want to project that elusive characteristic called "executive presence." When I ask them what they mean, they usually give me a list that includes some of the following:

- An air of confidence

- Great eye contact

- Modulating voice volume

- Dynamic use of hands and facial expressions

- Superior posture

I have the same solution every time. I tell them to paint a picture with their words. Here's my explanation. When you are taking the time to paint a picture of any scene—a meeting, an event, a celebration, or a failure—and are describing it through actions and objects, you'll automatically do all the right things, physically.

Your sincere description will automatically give you great eye contact, voice modulation, expressions, movements, and posture. You will not even think about it but just become more compelling naturally, as you paint your picture. That all adds up to being a confident, dynamic communicator who is a force to be reckoned with. That is executive presence. And it's yours right now. Just follow the protocol we've been discussing: Make your clear and direct opening statement, follow it with a picture that incorporates the rule of three, and they'll be listening to you. They also may give you that back-handed compliment: "Wow, what did you eat for breakfast this morning?"

This is a great moment for you, so fight the urge to become defensive. Take the mild slap ("You were a boring communicator before, but now you are interesting!") in stride. Smile. And tell them you'll have a lot more great ideas in the days and weeks ahead. They'll look forward to listening to you. You'll be succeeding. And you'll like it.

Let's now revisit our poster children—Sheila, David, and Linda—and incorporate in the power of pictures in their attempts to connect with their audiences. Please count the objects and actions in the picture of each scenario.

Example: Sheila

In Chapter 3 we gave Sheila the additional agenda sentences that will set the scene for her picture:

> "Our line of credit comes up for review in a couple of weeks, and the way our business is growing, we're going to need an increase. I've already talked to the bank and they say it won't be an issue based on our profits, which are way ahead of last year's. All they need to see is the third-quarter Profit and Loss statement when I meet with them on Thursday. Can you have it to me by Wednesday so I can review it before I go into my meeting?"

Now let's add a picture that will drive the message home to Josh:

> "I know that when the loan officer looks over our financials he'll see we've done a great job of blowing through our projections. This will be good news for him because he'll be able to scoot this loan request through his underwriters without a drop of sweat. He'll look good, get the loan approved, and we'll get the money we need to fund those projects we need to grow. But it all starts with you getting those numbers to me."

Josh should be getting the message by now, because Sheila has done a great job of connecting. That clear and well-painted picture of the loan officer approving the loan should be the nice little pick-me-up and career motivator that Josh needs to get cracking. The company needs his expertise and efforts to move forward. If he's still not getting it, Sheila will realize Josh is not the right one to turn to for help and she'll know to not waste the effort in the future. By committing the time and effort to setting her communication agenda and then painting a powerful picture, Sheila is creating an environment in which Josh can succeed.

Example: David

Here are the agenda sentences we gave David to help him succeed with his real estate idea:

> "This company will grow quickly if we look at growing markets that could use what we sell. I'd like our group to spend some minimal time and money examining this health-care idea. If my gut feeling is right, we can take our current products, and with minor tweaking, sell them to a whole new customer base. It's could be a great way to grow our company. I need the help of each of you to see if my idea has legs, and so I'm going to make a request of each of you."

Now, let's give him some more ammunition that will make his requests of Susan, Denise, and Phil more compelling:

> "The real estate professionals are constantly searching for a leg up on the competition, and I'll bet we can give them something they can't get anywhere else. This is an industry where everyone talks to everyone else about what ideas work. They're

constantly networking and burning up the phone lines. If we can strike now we can make our mark quickly, and boost our revenues without spending a ton of money."

David's idea may or may not have legs, but Susan, Denise, and Josh have a lot more reasons now to get behind doing the homework David is asking for. And it's all because David spent the extra 160 words or so to set the agenda *and* paint a quick picture of the real estate community beating a path to his company's door. It is a great use of his time.

Example: Linda

We forced Linda to take a break from her "ingredient once-over" so she could spell out why she needs that extra condensed milk.

> "Everyone loves those "Hello Dollies," especially your Mother. They will all be disappointed if they don't turn out right, and I can see right now I'm short the two cans of condensed milk that the recipe calls for. That condensed milk is the secret ingredient. Without two more cans my favorite recipe is in trouble."

Now let's give her the sentences to make it memorable to her partner:

> "My favorite part of the whole meal is serving those "Hello Dollies." I love seeing all three generations—from your Mom, to you and your brother Barry, to our kids and their cousins—grabbing at the tray of "Hello Dollies." I'll put out the traditional pumpkin pie and whipped cream, but everyone always saves room for our "Hello Dollies." I can't prepare them properly without the condensed milk. Please pick up to extra cans

for me . . . I need them at least two hours before everyone gets
here."

Even an unconscious husband will remember the condensed
milk after this wonderful generational portrait that Linda paints.
If this is all it takes to get everyone together in such a Normal
Rockwell moment, most of us would run right out and buy several cases of condensed milk. The key to the success of Linda's
new communication is that she is working to connect with her
husband about something she strongly believes in. By taking the
extra effort, Linda has made her husband realize how important
the "Hello Dollies" are to her and to making the holiday feast a
success, and in the process she has become a much stronger
communicator.

Observation Assignment

During the next few days, pinpoint how many times someone
uses a word picture to make a point. Listen to a couple of examples, and watch for how the more the speaker "puts you there"
by painting the picture, the more interesting, funnier, or more
poignant what they are describing becomes.

Also notice how the speakers are subtly effecting change and
that it's all about you: making you laugh, giving you understanding you didn't have, and getting you to think a little more deeply
about a certain topic.

But don't limit observations to work: Listen to everybody.
Maybe the guy at the convenience store is telling a clever story,
or your neighbor has something to share about work. Listen to
their techniques and see whether they are painting a picture with
their words, or just reciting facts.

CHAPTER 5

How to Make Boring Jargon and Stats Fascinating

YOU'LL FIND THAT PAINTING A PICTURE with your words is going to do a lot for you, in the office and at home. Now its time to learn how to work these dynamic word pictures into your everyday meetings and conversations. You will do it by making unimaginative industry references, acronyms, and statistics come alive. Like most "It" factor skills, this will involve more effort from you. However, it will be a rewarding effort and a good investment of your brain power.

This chapter is the natural follow-up to the "grab a bite" vs. "herb-crusted salmon" exercise. Relying on boring statistics, overused expressions, or industry jargon, which dominate so many of our meetings, is running on a straight path to mediocrity. Superior communicators understand that nobody pays much attention to average communication. Average is forgettable. We do pay attention to unique and dynamic word pictures that make an impact and build fast connections.

So, let's unveil this tactical strategy. (Or I could say, strategic tactic, as a way of mocking "I'm smart" business-speak?) Be it tactic or strategy, let's learn to eliminate mediocrity by using powerful, customized, and memorable word pictures.

You show you "belong at the table" when you make the industry jargon *come alive with pictures*. The typical lazy communicator uses industry jargon instead of going to the trouble of explaining the importance or relevance of the jargon. Lots of participants in my workshops tell me they think it's important to use industry jargon, especially with prospective clients, because they think it establishes credibility.

I tell them they are only half right. It establishes something all right: insecurity.

If you constantly interject jargon, then it sends a clear message that you are not an expert, but an aspiring wannabe. If you beef up and bolster that jargon up by painting a picture of the reason you threw out the jargon, you're starting to sound like you know what you're talking about and that you belong in the room.

Of course, you need to understand the jargon and be able to use it intelligently. Just don't rely on it to make you sound credible. It won't. The goal of attaining "It" is to create a positive impression with your words and thoughts, not merely to mimic overused bromides.

Let's take a simple bit of jargon from the banking industry. If you've ever applied for a small business loan, during the closing process your smiling banker will have asked you to sign several pages called "the U.C.C."

"Hey," you ask, "What's this?"

"Oh, that," says the banker, "It's the Uniform Commercial Code document. It's just something you have to sign to get the loan."

"Yeah, okay, but what is it?" you ask, being a very reasonable person. "Oh, well," says the banker, smiling an all-knowing smile. "This document perfects the credit."

"Really," you say, not yet realizing that the banker is being lazy, "so this is going to help my credit score? Funny, I thought it was already pretty good. I don't understand. Besides, I thought this whole thing was based on my company's performance, not my personal credit."

"Well, no," says the banker, still smiling, "this document perfects the credit for our records and files."

This discussion could go on for at least another five minutes, with the banker throwing out description after description of this U.C.C. document without you ever understanding what it really is, or why on earth you have to sign it.

Eventually you will sign it, because you can't get the loan without it, but the banker is missing a great opportunity to connect with you and perhaps earn a referral.

A banker who is a good strong communicator (I've heard the good ones are!) would work harder and come up with something like this:

"This document that we're both signing is part of the long-standing Uniform Commercial Code. It's a document that bankers and their customers use across the country. It's going to go on file as a public document with the Secretary of State in our state capitol in (Albany, Sacramento, etc.). It's important because it's a formal record that we've loaned you money and that you promise to pay it back or forfeit the collateral you've put up for the loan, which in this case is your beach condo. We can't make any business loans without it. It's a critical part of the banking process. Both of us have to be willing to report to the state government that we've entered into this agreement, otherwise the banking system would never work."

Wow, you think. This is a banker who not only wants my business but is willing to take the time to help me understand the whole process. This is someone I like and with whom I'm going to keep doing business. In fact, I'm going to tell my friends.

Here's another reason this description of the ever-present U.C.C. is effective. It specifically spells out the responsibility of each party in this business relationship. The bank gives you the money, you pay it back or lose your beach condo. There's no reason for the banker to avoid mentioning this responsibility, because that's also what it says in the loan documents. Better to hit this straight on and discuss the purpose of the document while demonstrating respect for the customer and help him or her understand what the thick stack of papers known as the U.C.C. is all about.

For the banker willing to take the trouble to paint a picture of the document going on file at the state capital, instead of just throwing out snippets of meaningless jargon, the effort pays off: a stronger, respectful connection with a good customer who will turn into a source of referrals.

Sometimes, sadly, we use industry jargon to try to sound smart, or as smart as others in the room (I've done it too, I admit!). If you're trying to sound smart or superior, jargon is a losing tool. Everyone sniffs out your weakness sooner or later, after which you'll never be taken seriously.

Bankers take heart. This same rule applies to every profession on the planet. Jargon words, taken literally for their pop culture value and meaning, become silly, as I delight in pointing out:

• Information technology consultants have all those crazy "enterprise solutions," which have nothing to do with Captain

Kirk, nor with Scotty, who episode after episode are always "giving it all we've got, Jim."

• Accountants love to toss around "generally accepted accounting principles," which make me wonder about the underdogs. You know, the "less than generally accepted principles." Why did those principles miss the cut? Will they ever find general acceptance? Are they seeking therapy to deal with their acceptance issues?

• Human Resources professionals will tell you how many new hires they are "on-boarding" this quarter. What a cool company, I think . . . a cruise for all new employees!

• Environmental engineers will go on and on about the "migration" of contaminants, and there's never a mallard or goose in sight headed for Canada. After that they'll launch right into "remedial" measures, when it seems to me that everyone in the room can read at about the same speed.

• Investment bankers must have an unspoken code that they have to spout the acronym "EBITDA" (pronounced ee-bit-duhh) no more than five minutes after stepping into every conference room they enter. For good measure they will throw in "earnings before interest, taxes, depreciation, and amortization" for the dullards in the room like me. Wow, somebody is proud of their MBA!

• Lawyers are the first to admit they are easy targets in this game. Still the grade school kid in me always chuckles when a lawyer mentions filing an appellate brief, and I conjure the image of someone sorting their undergarment drawer to figure out the right thing to wear to the appellate court.

All of these professionals, like the banker with the simple definition of the U.C.C., are accurate and, on the surface, efficient, as they use the verbal tools of their trades ad nauseam. But they should not believe for a minute that it makes them effective or memorable communicators. All it means is that they've picked up a few industry words along the way and can toss them out as needed. This is lackluster communication at best, and irritating at the worst.

Now that you're getting used to this take on the senselessness of industry nano-speak, let's really dive into some conversations and help the speaker connect better with everyone in the room.

Here are some examples of glib industry jargon, some of which hold true for more than one industry. Each example is followed by a sarcastic retort that shows the facetiousness of the jargon, which is then followed by a picture of what that same jargon really means to the listener. The jargon is always easier to use, takes up less time, but in the end is meaningless.

Industry: Construction and Building

Glib and Meaningless Jargon: "We're proud to say we are a *fully integrated firm.*"

Sarcastic Retort: "Hey, I'm happy for you, but you aren't a little behind the times bragging about that? All strong companies are have been fully integrated for a long time now, so you sound ridiculous bringing up the fact you've got professionals other than white males working for you. I don't mean to tell you how to run your business, but shouldn't you use more relevant words like 'respecting diversity' instead?"

The Same Jargon Enhanced by Painting a Picture: "We're proud to say we are a fully integrated firm. That means we've got architects, construction professionals, and development experts right in the same office, working together as a team. When you hire us, you're saving time and money because the company that creates your design, builds your building, finds your land, and even helps with the bank financing is all a part of the same team. It's a great combination."

Industry: Business Consulting

Glib and Meaningless Jargon: "We're proud to say we are the type of firm constantly searching for *best practices* to put at your disposal."

Sarcastic Retort: "Great! But, are there any other types of practices you'd put at my disposal? Are there clients who pay you less than me, who get the average practices at their disposal? Do you make worst practices available to your clients who don't pay you in a timely manner?"

The Same Jargon Enhanced by Painting a Picture: "We're proud to say we are the type of firm constantly searching for *best practices* to put at your disposal. That means we're going to be able to save you a lot of time and money. We're constantly studying what the successful companies in your business are doing. We're going to show you the best ideas we find in our homework and help you pick the ones best suited to help your business grow. You will get the benefit of all of the research that everyone in our firm has done, as we sit down and decide together what is going to be best for you."

Industry: Property and Casualty Insurance

Glib and Meaningless Jargon: "Rest assured, we're going to contact the best carriers to find out who's going to write this policy."

Sarcastic Retort: "Hey, don't run up the bill on me. You don't have to write anything for me . . . no need to re-invent the wheel. Just go out find a policy that already exists. And, by the way, I don't need any help with my travel plans. I already have an awesome travel agent who gets me the best prices from all the air carriers. So you can cross that right off your list."

The Same Jargon Enhanced by Painting a Picture: "Rest assured, we're going to contact the best carriers to find out who's going to write this policy. That means we're going to be sending out a lot of e-mails and making a lot of telephone calls to a wide variety of insurance companies. With that information we'll do some comparisons to get you the right policy and the right protection for you at the right prices. There are lots of options out there, and we're going to find the best one for you. We want you to concentrate on running business. You'll sleep at night, knowing you're well covered by the policy we find for you.

These are just three examples. There are at least three million out there. And that's just mentioning the mild buzzwords. The list is even longer when you add industry acronyms and product model numbers. The rules are the same. Whenever you mention jargon, industry acronyms, or product model numbers, work hard to paint a picture to give it meaning. Otherwise, you're just providing a fact or a bit of information and your chances of effecting the change you desire have dropped considerably.

A common response of many to this call for hard work is to claim that this amounts to "dumbing things down." That's the sound of arrogance rearing its foolish head again. You build powerful connections when you use pictures to make jargon and acronyms come alive. Using jargon without memorable word pictures is like saying, "I use that word, so I'm really, really a smart person and I deserve to be in this conversation."

To make powerful connections, always sound as if you're talking to a friend or a neighbor whom you respect. That means being mindful of jargon at all times, not letting it flow out of your mouth in rapid succession, and instead going the extra mile and adding those few sentences that will help everyone in the room feel connected to you.

Powerful Pictures Trump Popular Business Clichés

"Business smart-speak" or lame clichés are more irritating than industry jargon. These ubiquitous words and catch phrases make speakers sound as if they are manipulating us, hoping to sound cool and smart, but not saying anything substantive. There are lots of books and websites devoted to the silliness of these inane business-isms. Here let's focus on the harm they will do you if you keep incorporating them into your conversations.

I say, just *be cool and smart* by dumping the clichés and replacing them with pictures you paint about what you're talking about. Let's go through the same discipline as we did with jargon.

- *Stomach-Turning Cliché:* Matrix-Driven Organization

If this is supposed to be impressive, rest assured it's not, especially when a Wisenheimer like me says to himself, "Matrix driven, that's awesome! I loved every one of those movies, especially the woman with the short hair and all that leather!"

"Matrix-driven" may be accurate, but it's weak, mail-order MBA talk. When you rely on what you think are smart-sounding catch phrases, you'll be lumped in with the shallow wannabes. "We measure everything we do" is a good phrase to replace "matrix-driven organization," but it's still too a brief description and not the picture we're looking for. Let's take another crack at this label, and make it work with a picture:

"We measure everything we do. Every sales person has to grade every single meeting they have in terms of whether this fits into our industry mix and geographic reach. We report those

grades every Wednesday in the conference room. That way we can keep track of our pipeline and what's going to work for us and what won't. Now our sales team is developing a great track record of predicting success."

This is much more accurate, dynamic, and helpful. The listener doesn't even have to worry about the exact meaning of the words "matrix-driven" and can instead concentrate on connecting to the speaker, who is obviously working hard to build that connection.

Let's quickly examine some other turn-offs:

• *Stomach-Turning Cliché:* "We partner with our clients to become a virtual extension of their staff."

Sarcastic Retort: "Really? Then I guess you don't ever send them a bill. Partners usually don't bill each other. As a virtual extension of their staff, do you receive virtual health-care benefits?"

Better with a Picture: "We work hard to get to know our clients' businesses very well. We not only pore over industry Internet sites and publications, but we go out and spend time, in person, with their customers. We'll have coffee and bagels in their break rooms, grab a deli sandwich, or set up dinner meetings to find out exactly how our clients are succeeding and how they can do better. All that research helps us to find out things about our clients that they do not even know."

• *Stomach-Turning Cliché:* "Our market is comprised of C-level decision makers."

Sarcastic Retort: "Too bad you're not doing better. I prefer working with the top of the heap, you know, the A-type decision makers. Maybe a B-level guy every now and then to round things out, but I usually like the A-level guys the best. Too bad you can't work your way past the C-level guys."

Better with a Picture: "We only pitch our programs to senior managers and executives. These are the bosses who have the most investment and stock on the line. That means we only go after people like the chairman, president, and chief financial officer, who can pull the trigger quickly on our detailed proposals and get us hired.

Please notice that you don't need to draw a lengthy picture to get you connected. Just follow the protocol of the simple declarative sentence, some powerful action words, and some easy-to-visualize objects:

- Pull the trigger on our detailed proposals
- Coffee and bagels in the break room
- We report those grades every Wednesday

So make sure you are always painting vibrant pictures—even in just a single phrase—instead of trying to sound like a hot shot.

Never Let a Number Stand Alone: Back It Up with a Picture

Numbers and statistics stand in the way of the connection process. They will hamper and even block your efforts to connect with the audience. Although you may need to use statistics when you're talking, numbers and stats by themselves rarely help you connect with others. I look at them as a necessary evil. You can't get along in business or at home without them, but numbers and statistics also have the potential to stop every communication dead in its tracks.

Used incorrectly, numbers and stats are frequently the culprit when you find you just aren't connecting with the people who are most important to you. They have the potential to force listeners to stop listening to *you* and instead focus on the questions raised by the *numbers.*

- "Is this number right? It can't be!"
- "How did she come up with this number?"
- "Is this number a lot, or a little?"
- "How does this number fit with the other five numbers she's just mentioned? I'd better turn back two pages in this report and do some figuring of my own."

You can't stop entirely all these internal questions, but you can help the listeners to put them aside. All it takes is (you guessed it!) more effort on your part as you give your numbers and stats meaning and relevance.

If you can't tell your listeners why they should care about the numbers or statistics you so proudly put in front of them, don't use them. When you do use numbers and stats, be sure to back them up by painting a picture that will make them come to life. Let's go through several examples, showing the difference between using numbers alone and numbers with a picture:

Example #1: The Financial Report

Using Numbers Alone That Force Disconnecting Questions:

> "Our gross margin last quarter peaked at 37 percent. We need to be at 41 percent."

Using Numbers with a Picture, Following the Picture-Painting Rules:

> Our gross margin last quarter peaked at 37 percent. This improvement is good news for us, but it's not good enough. For

us to hit our profit goals we're going to have to work even harder at increasing our productivity internally or get some better prices from our suppliers. I'm going to meet with the warehouse crew this afternoon to get their ideas on how to speed thing up, and Rhonda already has been on the phone today with our suppliers, asking for an across-the-board cut in prices, in return for our speeding up payment terms. We will pick up the extra four points we need in the gross margin in the next quarter."

Analysis: This number (37 percent), backed up by all those action words and objects, now has meaning and relevance. There may be subsequent debate about the methods proposed to increase the gross margin, but the numbers have given the proposed change meaning. And a good thing for the speaker is that this use of the number hasn't caused her audience to drift off, because the two pictures have them focusing on her issue. The speaker has them talking about what she wants to talk about: the importance of increasing the margin. Also, she did the math for her colleagues: "We will pick up the extra four points we need in the gross margin in the next quarter."

When you introduce numbers, you introduce math. Try to do as much of the math as possible ahead of time, so your listeners can concentrate on your message rather than on your calculations. This was a real point of connection for the speaker. Her extra 98 words gave her executive presence. That was worth the time and energy she spent.

Example #2: The Job Offer

Using Numbers Alone That Force Disconnecting Questions:
    "I'm happy to offer you a position with our firm, with a starting salary of $56,500. Welcome."

Using Numbers with a Picture, Following the Picture-Painting Rules:
    "I'm happy to offer you a position with our firm, with a start-

ing salary of $56,500. We've done our homework, and we know that this offer stacks up very well in our industry for a strong applicant with your experience and training. But this is just the start. I look forward to sitting down with you, right here at my desk, for your first performance review in six months. That will be in April. If your performance is as impressive as I hope it will be, we'll be discussing a raise. Welcome!"

Analysis: Discussing pay is always tough, so this is one of the roughest numbers to have to deal with. It can be emotional, contentious, and a real sticking point for both the boss and the applicant who may want to work together very much. Few people who are offered jobs ever say, "Oh, that's too much, really. I'd be much happier working for less. Please cut the offer right now or I won't accept."

The boss can cut the tension immediately by focusing on what the number represents, not on the number itself. The offer is the offer, and in this case, the boss gives the number meaning and relevance by painting the picture of the "homework." The second picture involves that number of $56,500 going up, at the hoped-for positive performance review. No promises, but an optimistic picture of tomorrow. These extra 75 words can do a lot for the boss by convincing the applicant to accept the position quickly and start the job with a good attitude.

* * * * * *

Making jargon and statistics come alive, while avoiding trendy business-speak, will always mean a little more work, energy, and preparation for you. You will get used to it. Besides, it's the only way to get "It."

Observation Assignment

The best way to stop your use of jargon is to study how it limits others in their communication efforts. At your next meeting, perhaps this week, use hash marks to keep a running total of how many times your colleagues throw out a number or use a piece of jargon, which could be bolstered by a connective picture.

But remember to be fair in your tally: It's not always necessary to add the word picture. Instead, concentrate on the times your colleagues are not connecting as much as they should because they are taking short cuts instead of giving value to their jargon or numbers.

CHAPTER 6

Preserve Your Hard-Won Connections by Avoiding Patronizing Patter

NO MATTER HOW MANY MILES YOU RUN A WEEK, how many spinning classes you take, or how much time you spend on the treadmill, you're not going to get your twenty-one-year-old waistline back if you finish every workout with a plate of Twinkies and a 22-ounce Mountain Dew. You've ruined your work-out.

It's the same with your communication efforts. Don't ruin all the good will and great connections you've been forging by saying something patronizing, insulting, or out-and-out moronic.

The warning is necessary because it happens all the time. And sadly, those spoiling their communication efforts are never aware of how they have hurt themselves. This chapter will be devoted to identifying those expressions that destroy connections.

This is a change of gears. During the last five chapters we have been concentrating on adding words, sentences, and entire paragraphs to your arsenal as you develop your personal connection skills. It takes more words and more effort to tell people what your agenda is and then paint dynamic pictures to make that agenda come alive. Those extra sentences and paragraphs are going to help you succeed in every meeting.

I've encouraged you to say more and not to worry about taking extra time. Now I want you to cut back on some of the things you are saying that are hurting you—not to save time, but to save your winning connections. You are now ready to study and recognize the evil words, sentences, and expressions you must eliminate so you don't ruin everything you've been working for.

Patronizing, off-hand sentence fillers, which you may not even think about as you say them, can be disastrous for you. You can paint a great picture that literally compels others to listen to you, and then break that magic connection by dumping out a communication killer that you don't even recognize. These dastardly words and expressions are so ubiquitous they seem harmless. They aren't.

Let me paint a picture for you. You are successfully combining every ounce of wit, charm, and grace you possess at your next dinner party: taking a turn at the piano playing "Hey Jude" and other Beatles favorites, complimenting the hostess on her successful integration of eclectic design motifs, and chatting with the teenage son about the ins and outs of the X-Box game "Halo." You are on fire with your connections, and it's a good time. But you are not home free.

If you off-handedly remark to the hostess as she serves you another appetizer, "Those are beautiful slacks. Did they fit when you bought them?" you have flushed all your charisma down the drain. You are an insensitive jerk, plain and simple, and nobody will remember your entire Beatles repertoire.

You may protest that you would never be so blatantly insulting and insensitive, and I agree. It's an exaggeration. But you are probably insulting others on a regular basis in a more subtle way that in the long run is just as hurtful. You just don't realize it. You may never directly insult a gracious hostess, but there's a good chance you're using words, phrases, and expressions that are subtly insulting and slowly yet methodically undermining your credibility and connections.

I see it all the time. Powerful communications are killed by gratuitous remarks. The sad thing is that the communication sinner doesn't even know or understand the nature of the sin. Because so many of us commit these communication sins all the time, it may not seem like a bad thing. But it is.

Some of the communication killers I'm going to enumerate have actually come out of my mouth in the past and still slip out every now and then. It's impossible to cleanse yourself of them every moment of every day. But I don't let the everyday nature of these expressions fool me, and neither should you. This chapter will teach you to be aware of the dastardly effects of the patronizing communication words and how to rid yourself of the harmful words.

We're going to methodically go through the communication killer *Eight Deadly Sins*, detailing the destructive nature of each. At first glance, you may argue, "Well that word isn't so bad," or "I never took that to be a negative." You have been fooled by their subtlety and popularity. It's time to wake up.

These are words and expressions you are going to recognize in your own speech patterns every day. There's no particular order here and there are many more you may want to add to your own personal list. But if you expunge these expressions from every conversation you have from this day forward, you'll be better off for it. So will everyone who hears the sound of your voice.

Patronizing Communication Sin #1
Misuse of the Word "Certainly"

If you use the word "certainly" *only* to answer a yes-or-no question with a positive, direct, and upbeat emphasis, you are one of the rare communications superstars.

If you are using "certainly" in any other situation as an attempt to demonstrate warmth or intensity, you are, sadly, creating a subtle yet nefarious communications disconnect.

Don't despair; you are in good company. The rich, the not rich, the urban, the suburban, the rural—they all use "certainly" as an adverb, usually with unfortunate results. If you're a member of this ill-advised adverb pack, you think the word "certainly" strengthens sentences. It doesn't. Instead it demonstrates passive-aggressive, manipulative, and weak behavior worthy of a dysfunctional guest on *Dr. Phil*. Even worse, it shows you just don't care enough to put forth the effort to communicate with power. Misuse of the word "certainly" kills connections.

- *Exhibit A:* "We *certainly* are glad to be here today."

"Certainly" adds nothing here but a healthy dose of insincerity. The sentence is more meaningful without it. If you were "certainly" glad to be here, you'd go to more trouble and say why. For example:

Stronger Communication Without "Certainly":

"We are glad to be here today because we enjoy spending time with you."

Or:

"We are glad to be here today because you always make us feel so welcome."

- *Exhibit B:* "I *certainly* do appreciate your business."

See Exhibit A and add a dose of "Eddie Haskell, party of one, your table is now ready." If you "certainly" do appreciate your customer's business, you'd say why instead of just going through the motions of tossing in a meaningless adverb to make yourself sound like a great person when all you're accomplishing is adding "suck-up" to your resume.

Stronger Communication Without "Certainly":

"We appreciate your business. Lots of companies would like to work with you, and I'm glad you chose us. Thank you."

Or:

"We appreciate your business. Your projects are exciting, and working with you helps to make us more successful. Thank you."

- *Exhibit C:* "I *certainly* hope your report will be on time this week."

Yikes . . . are you trying to talk down to your employees and have them question your leadership abilities? If not, get rid of the judgmental "certainly" and be more direct.

Stronger Communication Without "Certainly":

"I'm counting on you. Please get the report to me on time this week."

It hurts you every time you use certainly as an adverb. So end the practice right now! Use "certainly" only as an answer to a yes-or-no question, and you'll stay golden.

Patronizing Communication Sin #2 "I Don't See Why Not"

Being direct and strong is the key to building strong connections. You are not furtive, clever, or shrewd when you seek to "cover your rear" while you deftly dodge the issue that's in front of everyone. Instead, you sound sneaky or weak. Both kill connections.

Trying to weasel out of a commitment with your words casts

instant doubts on your credibility and trustworthiness. It's devastating. And it all starts innocently enough.

Let's take a look at destruction in action. Your client gives you a call asking whether the project you are working on for her will be ready next week to meet their deadline. A lot is riding on your work, and she wants to make sure you will deliver.

She goes through the initial pleasantries and then pops the question, "Will you deliver on Thursday as promised?"

"Oh, right, next Thursday," you say, "Well, I don't see why not."

It sounds harmless but instead it's destructive. You have created tremendous doubt in her mind about your commitment to her project, and all because you thought you could outfox her. "Yes," "No," or "I don't know" are all better answers, and would help her do her job. Instead, you've chosen to be vaguely optimistic and noncommittal. You've covered your rear. You may be proud of yourself, but everyone loses when the words, "I don't see why not" come out of your mouth. Especially you!

The big problem with this is that it fails on many levels. She's not going to hold you any less accountable, even if she accepts your dodge. If next Thursday comes and you have not delivered she's still gong to be furious. You could protest that you never really promised you'd deliver on time, reminding her of your last phone conversation:

> "What I said was, I don't see why not, but at that time I didn't know that some of our suppliers were falling behind. And since they didn't deliver to me, I couldn't deliver to you. So really, you shouldn't be disappointed in me . . . not at all! I never really promised you, I just said I was hopeful."

But this explanation only makes a bad situation worse. I've never seen this weak dodge work. The client will be mad, and she may never forget that you let her down. The salt on the wound is the fervent reminder that you never committed to her, which just reinforces your cowardly position.

"Well, I don't see why not" never gives you the out you think it does. And worse than that, it creates distrust. Even if you think you are being crafty, everyone will hear your gutless answer, and it will register. At best, they'll subconsciously file away that you are not to be trusted. At worst, they'll heat things up with the direct challenge, "You don't see why not? What the hell does that mean? I can't go one step forward with you giving me a weak answer like that. We're depending on you. So get off the fence. Yes or no?"

There are better alternatives once you decide to be direct and strong instead of always covering your rear. If your client's question is "yes," tell her so, and then paint a picture of how things are progressing:

> "Yes, everything is on schedule. We've got the preliminary work all done, and now we're just putting on the final touches. We had a meeting in the conference room yesterday and several of our employees working on other projects stopped in to add some extra touches. I look forward to showing everything to you."

The "yes" news is easy to deliver. If the answer is "no," tell her so and paint a picture of what you're doing about it:

> "No, we're behind schedule. I've got the whole team working on Saturday to catch up, and I'll be right next to them all day. We'll be here Sunday, eating more delivery pizza, if we have to. We won't make the deadline, but we may be able to deliver 24 hours after that. I'll know more on Saturday night. May I

e-mail you or leave a voice mail to let you know where we
stand?"

This is not good news, but it's the type of communication
that builds connections. You've admitted you will be late, and
you've described what you are going to do about it. Any reasonable person would appreciate your directness about their important project, and most likely thank you for the update. Your client
won't be pleased, but because of your powerful connection it
won't hurt your relationship.

If the answer is "I don't know," tell her so, and paint a picture of the obstacles that stand in the way and what you're doing
about it:

"I don't know, because we're waiting for one more set of mate-
rials before we put everything together. I'll have an update by
3 P.M. today. Can I call you then and let you know whether we
are on track?"

Not perfect news, but it's a strong connection because you
set a specific deadline when you will know, and now she can
make plans.

I understand you may not always choose the directness of
"Yes, No, or I don't know"—for any number of reasons. I'm in
the same boat. But I just want you to consider carefully the price
you may pay when you use evasive words.

"I don't see why not" has lots of dirty little relatives, as they
will hurt you just as much. Here's my short list of "cover your
rear" words that can ruin your credibility. Look at this list and
use the family barometer to see if they pass muster. None of
them do, but let's go through this humorous exercise to help
convince you to fight the good fight to avoid these expressions:

- *"As far as I know . . ."*

"Grandma, the kids are looking forward to seeing you and Grandpa this weekend . . . as far as I know."

- *"For the most part . . ."*

"Honey, now that we've finally got a moment to ourselves during our thirtieth anniversary party, I can tell you that I always have and I always will adore you . . . for the most part."

- *"I hope. . . ."*

"Sweetheart, you have been so brave, while we've been waiting for the doctor . . . braver than most five-year-olds would be. And when he looks inside your ear to see if your infection has gone away, it won't hurt too much . . . I hope."

If the dodge doesn't sound right in a touching situation with one of your family members, don't use it anywhere else either.

Eliminating these vague modifiers may prove to be the toughest test in this chapter. Side-stepping commitment by covering your rear is easy, fast, and always takes less energy than being direct. But don't give in to the ease and seductiveness of this sin. The expression "I don't see why not" and its relatives will hurt you every time you use them.

Patronizing Communication Sin #3
"More than Happy" Is More Than Creepy

I'm completely stumped when someone tells me they'd be "more than happy" to do something. After five years of college and twenty years in the business world, I still don't know what it means, and so all I can do is guess. If you tell me you're *more than happy,* that leaves me wondering whether you are:

- Ecstatic?

- Elated?

- Euphoric?

- Overjoyed?

- Exuberant?

- Beside yourself with an overwhelming sense of near-narcotic well-being?

All this mirth coming from the guy at the hotel front desk just because I asked him to have another blanket sent up to my room? It all sounds not only creepy, but over the top. I say you're either happy to take care of this for me or you aren't. Adding that you are *more than* happy doesn't give you any additional power or connection to me.

Instead, the words "more than happy" can create a subliminal voice of mistrust between us, like you're goofing on me: "Sure hotshot, I'd be *more than happy* to bring a marvelous person like you a stinking blanket. We couldn't have Mister Wonderful do without being all warm and snuggly tonight, now could we?"

Drop "more than happy." It takes no effort and does possible harm. Instead let "happy" stand on its own, and add a sentence or two with an action verb that demonstrates that you are actually happy to complete the assigned task. Here are three examples:

- "I'd be happy to bring you cream. I'm heading for the kitchen right now."

- "I'd be happy to send you the report. As soon as we're finished with this call, I'll attach the report to an e-mail and have it heading your way in a minute."

- I'd be happy to look into your insurance issue. I have a friend in human resources whom I'll call right now. She should be able to get us an answer by tomorrow.

Now that I've alerted you to the dangers of "more than happy," I also want you to be cautious with "really" and "so very much." I'll keep this brief, because these two have a lot in common with "more than happy." They aren't as dastardly patronizing, but they rarely help your communication efforts.

I believe "I love you" is stronger than, "I *really* love you." I also believe 'I love you" is stronger than "I love you *so very much.*" Neither adds power or connection. They only insert a slight and subtle doubt into what should be a touching moment. "Really" and "so very much" can create a lot of trouble for you because they beg the question, why is it necessary to add to, or modify, "love?" Here are two sarcastic examples:

- "I know this is going to be difficult to believe, seeing as how I'm so great, and you're, well, not that wonderful. But, nonetheless, I really love you."

- "I love you so very much. This despite the fact we both know I can't help but pursue every single skirt that enters my peripheral vision."

"Really" and "so very much" aren't communications killers, but they undermine your strength and conviction, and that makes them dangerous. As difficult as it may be, try to rid yourself of them.

Patronizing Communication Sin #4
Saying "I Am Sorry" When You Are Not Sorry

There are two types of "false sorry-ers" (a new word!). One is the weak communicator who professes to be sorry because he believes it will help him in an upcoming confrontation. The other is the weak communicator who thinks she is being charming and coquettish with the smiling repetition of "I'm sorry." Both damage hard-won connections. Here is the simple rule: Don't say you are "sorry" when you aren't.

You can smell the dishonesty in the room when someone says in a harsh tone, "Well, I'm sorry, but I just have to disagree." You know they aren't sorry at all. They are indignant, furious, upset. And that's okay, because it's strong direct communication. But they aren't sorry, at all! You're sure of that. And that's not okay, because they are not being direct. Once they interject a facetious tone it hurts the whole connection process.

It's all very parental. "Well, I'm sorry, young man," the parent says, "but you are not leaving this house to go have a great time at the water park until that room is spotless." But Mom or Dad aren't sorry at all except over the fact they have to be the sole voice of reason in an unmanageable world. If that parental "I'm sorry" doesn't move you to rid of the words, let me try another voice for you. It's the cultured English film star from the 1950s—say, Basil Rathbone or Sir Alec Guinness—admonishing the eager-beaver American, "I'm sorry, old boy, but we really can't have that sort of business here, now can we?"

And that's the whole problem with the use of the put-down, "I'm sorry." The speaker is making it clear in condescending fashion that he is indeed sorry that he has to be the only clear thinker in the room.

There's no reason to say "I'm sorry." It would be so much better for everyone if these "false-sorryers" would just say what's on their minds, directly and sincerely:

- "I'm upset by your words, and I need to disagree."
- "Your ideas are not the right way for us to go, and it makes me angry that we are considering going down this road.

The benefit of such direct statements is they save everyone time, because you have eliminated the need for jockeying, jousting, and gamesmanship. Both parties know where you stand. The issues are on the table, including your displeasure. Real work can now begin to resolve the conflict without the mistrust and disconnect that a preemptive and hollow, "I'm sorry," would have triggered.

Now, let's go to a different use of "I'm sorry" that's more infuriating. It's the people who say they are sorry to interrupt the flow of a conversation, meeting, or presentation, but they just can't hold back their brilliant inquiry. They aren't sorry at all, but they want to make their interruption more palatable. It doesn't work. It's just irritating.

For example, in the sentence, "I'm sorry, but could I just ask you a question before we go any further?" the "I'm sorry" doesn't help at all. If you were sorry enough you wouldn't interrupt. You're not really sorry, you're just saying it to appear considerate, and as soon as everyone hears your question they'll be glad you interrupted.

A better way to handle your interruption is to be direct. It's also more respectful because you aren't breaking into a fake grovel. Here's how your interruption should sound:

"May I interrupt to ask a question?"

The current speaker can accede the floor to you ("Sure, go ahead and ask."), or not ("Could you please hold your question for a minute or two while I get through this point?"). Either way, when you ask for permission instead of offering a false apology, it creates a great connection. You're demonstrating interest and thoughtfulness. That's a winning communication technique.

Pardon the Interruption

Now a word about how to handle interrupting questions when you are the speaker. These interrupting questions should not be insulting or irritating, so don't be upset by them. As long as the questions are sincere, they are good news for you. It shows you have them listening to you, so much so that they want to add to the conversation, move it forward, or help define your thoughts. That doesn't mean you have to stop everything and answer them if it isn't the right time. But never show displeasure. Be polite and answer their question or ask them if you can return to their question in a few minutes.

Patronizing Communication Sin #5
Never Tell Others You Are Being "Honest"

We can quickly dispose of "honestly" and its evil dastardly cousins, "to tell you the truth" and "frankly." So here is the simple admonishment. May these words never leave your lips:

"Honestly . . ."

"To tell you the truth . . ."

"Frankly . . ."

Just because others use these expressions every day doesn't mean you should. Take a look at their literal interpretation:

"Honestly . . . because we both know my integrity is usually in doubt."

"To tell you the truth. . . . because I exaggerate incessantly."

"Frankly . . . because you know I can't stop from maliciously spreading lie after lie."

When you say "honestly," your listener consciously or unconsciously starts to wonder about you. Why do you have to say you're being honest? You shouldn't have to point it out . . . ever!

Many speakers default to "honestly," not because they are defensive about their integrity, but because they are lazy. They don't want to trouble themselves saying what they really mean, which probably is something like this:

- "This is going to be a difficult conversation."
- "This means a lot to me."
- "I'm passionate about this topic."
- "I want to share something important with you"
- "I'm worried I'm not connecting with you."

The integrity trio of "honestly," "frankly," and "to tell you the truth" can hurt you every single time you use them. Get rid of them. And then try not to wince the next time your boss decides to add gravity to her remarks by adding the words, "to tell you the truth."

Patronizing Communication Sin #6
"I'm Just Saying . . ." Means "I'm Just Criticizing You"

Sometimes we like to criticize people but want to remain pristine and cordial by pretending we haven't said anything critical at all. This is wimpy communication behavior and it hurts your credibility and current as well as future connections. Whenever you add, "I'm just saying," it's never preceded by a positive statement. It doesn't soften the blow. It makes it worse because of your "Hey, I'm a great guy" posturing. For example:

- *You may say:* "I think your budget projections are way off, but I'm just saying." *What the other person hears is:* "I think your budget projections are way off, but I'm just questioning your competence."

• *You may say:* "I don't think that tie goes with that shirt, but I'm just saying." *What the other person hears is:* "I don't think that tie goes with that shirt, but I'm just being obnoxious and critical."

I don't think it's possible to determine exactly when the expression "I'm just saying" became accepted as a free pass to criticize without consequence. It's a dark day in communication history because "I'm just saying" hurts someone else every time you use it.

A close relative is "just so you know," which doesn't work either. It's a weak way of patting yourself on the back. When someone says, "Just so you know, I'm not making a nickel on this deal," they are saying: "I'm helping you out. I'm a great person. You should applaud me."

If you want someone to know something, just tell him or her. If you feel the need to get praise, be more direct about it. "I'm doing you a favor" is more accurate, but lots of people think that's too boastful or direct. So they want to hint at it by saying, "just so you know." It's a weak disconnect. It does not help you to garner attention for your good actions.

So, make a decision: Come out and proclaim the benefits of whatever you've done or keep mum about how great you are. My guess is that you'll keep the congratulations to yourself and in the process maintain your great connection.

Patronizing Communication Sin #7
Repeat Often, Just Never Point Out That You Are Repeating

Great communicators repeat their key agenda items over and over again. When you have "It," you ignore that "Mommy and

Daddy" voice that tells you everybody is always listening to you. You know that because of all the competition for the attention of others, you have to keep repeating key agenda items over and over again.

Repetition works to help both the speaker and the listener focus on the business of connection. That's why repetition plays such a key role in prayer and liturgy, no matter what the religion. In classical music it's the coda, in pop music it's the hook. Repeating key ideas and thoughts and themes makes them memorable. Repetition is good.

That's why Mick Jagger mentions the word "satisfaction" eleven times in his and cowriter Keith Richard's ode to frustration. The song would never work with just a mention or two. Winning politicians at every level repeat their ideas and even their attacks at every rally and in every speech, as though it were the first time they said it.

Repetition is necessary. But drawing attention to your repetition is a quick way to aggravate your listeners and kill any headway you made toward making a connection.

"As I said before" sounds to others as if you are insinuating they may not have the intellect to catch on to what you are saying. It seems harmless enough because you are probably just giving yourself a gentle bit of reassurance out loud, "I'm okay here. I just said this. I'm on solid ground."

But that is not what the listeners hear. What they hear is that you are frustrated with them or that they just aren't smart enough to get your brilliance. Follow lead of the Rolling Stones. Never once in the historic three-minutes-and-thirteen-second cut recorded in Los Angeles over forty years ago did Mick Jagger use the words, "As I said before, I can't get no satisfaction." Be like Mick. Just say it again, without reminding us you're saying it again.

Patronizing Communication Sin #8
"Basically" Kills Every Sentence It Touches

If your goal is to get under the skin of the people you are talking to, make liberal use of the worthless word "basically." If that is not your purpose, get rid of it in your sentences. There is no reason to preface your comments with the message that you are "making it basic." That does not endear you to your listeners, who are wondering why you must tell them you are "making it basic" for them.

Speakers who can't get through ten words without a "basically" or two may be compensating for not being able to spit it out the way they want to. But instead of pausing to collect their thoughts (see the benefits of pausing in Chapter 4), they blurt out "basically" over and over again, distancing themselves from their audience every time.

"Basically" is a nine letter word that annihilates your connections. Dismiss it from your vocabulary.

Not Sins, but Irritating

Now I want to run through some expressions that may not destroy your communication efforts, but may be irritating to the ears of those you are trying so hard to connect with. So while we're getting rid of the sins, let's expunge these irritants as well.

"No Problem" Is a Big Problem

The hackneyed expression "no problem" is not a proper response when someone says, "thank you." Somewhere in the last twenty years, this bit of "I'm just a cool, laid-back dude" cadence has become a part of our daily conversations. So here's a good rule of thumb governing the usage of "no problem." If you:

- Are over 19

- Are not a surfer

- Do not have tanned skin and blond highlights from the sun

- Do not have washboard abs

then the proper response to "thank you" is "you're welcome." I'm not saying that "no problem" is never appropriate. It is the perfect response to soothe someone who is worried they have wronged you. Here's where "no problem" does work:

"Oh my gosh, I've spilled water all over your report."

"No problem. It cleaned up nicely. No harm done."

"I'm sorry I'm late for my appointment with you."

"No problem. I was able to take care of a few things while you made your way here."

"I forgot to send the attachment with the e-mail. I'm going to re-send it."

"No problem. I look forward to receiving it."

Here's a final test. When your boss beams, "Wow, great job on the marketing report. It makes my job so much easier. Thank you."—how do you respond? Answer: You respond with "Thank you." Do not say "No problem," even if you've got washboard abs.

"I'm Good" Is Not the Same as "No, Thank You"

If you are offered a beverage but wish to decline, please remember the host is not asking you about your state of mind or moral proclivity. The host wants to know whether you want something to drink, not your personal assessment of your character. By using the now ubiquitous "I'm good" you sound like you've just spent the afternoon with your self-affirmation coach.

The question "Are you thirsty?" and the retort "I'm good" do not intersect. You can be "good" or "fine" and still be thirsty. "I'm good" is the proper response when someone asks you how you are feeling, or how you are doing.

"Don't Go There" Is a Bad Place to Go

What a massive backward leap pop culture took in the last decade when "don't go there" became the hip and encouraged replacement phrase for "I don't want to discuss that subject," or "If we get further into that matter I will become angrier than I am now." Add the word "even" and a real fracas could be brewing: "Don't *even* go there!!"

Much better to pause and be direct. You will connect better if you refrain from this meaningless expression, which is probably a collective holdover from an exchange between Rachel and Phoebe in a 1997 episode of *Friends*.

Sports Analogies and References

Once in a while sports analogies are acceptable, but you won't hit a grand slam if you overuse them. I mean, the way to ace your connections is to make sure you are constantly following the communications playbook I've outlined. I know you need to score a touchdown with your communication efforts, but you'll never reach first base if you don't have some bench strength

Okay, that was facetious. Sports analogies are overused and consequently boring. And there is a segment of every audience that finds sports terminology meaningless, even when you think it is a slam dunk. (It's difficult to stop, once you start.) So I'd ask you to work harder to come up with more creative or descriptive expressions and just punt on the sports analogies. But then I'd be breaking my own rule.

Asking Questions You Then Answer Yourself

If you ask people a question, most normal folks would assume that you want them to answer it. So when you repeatedly ask a question and then answer it yourself, you give the impression that you are mildly psychotic or in love with your own eloquence. Consider the weirdness of the following soliloquy:

> "Why do I rail against asking questions that I myself then answer? I rail because it is an irritating practice. Am I happy about what I hear? Of course I am not. Can anything be done about it? Well, I certainly hope so. Why do I ask and then answer these questions? Because I think it makes me sound wise and Socratic. Does it accomplish that goal? Of course not." (In the spirit of full patronization, I threw in "certainly" for good measure.)

Questions are meant to be answered by someone other than you. Give someone else a chance to talk, and stifle your brilliance for just a minute or two.

First Person Always, Third Person Never

Since I have brought up borderline psychotic expressions, I'd like to counsel you against the irritating habit some people have of referring to themselves in the third person. It doesn't add impact. It adds discomfort.

Consider the statement: "No way Mark goes for that. No sir." Coming from me, these sentences should have you wondering whether I have a split personality and whether, under the proper psychiatric care, Mark will someday emerge again and perhaps be able to speak for himself. Why else would I talk about Mark as if he were not in the room? It's not effective, it's silly. Mark agrees.

"People Person" as Opposed to What?

It's cheap and mediocre to refer to yourself or someone else as "a real people person." I always wonder if that means the "people" person enjoys the company of humans instead of other species that roam the earth. You know, like the real red-headed woodpecker person or real moray eel person, who are both in my tennis club. It's just another lazy way of saying:

- This person is fun to be around.
- This person is easy to talk to.
- This person loves to meet new people.

Don't take the easy way out with your description of a vibrant, enthusiastic person. Work harder.

Be Consistent with the Good and the Bad

Communication superstars are known for being extremely consistent. Strive for that same consistency as you avoid lazy, common, and ultimately insincere and hurtful phrases. Instead add original, customized, and action-oriented phrases that make each of your statements and expressions distinctive. And then do it all day long, every day, over and over again.

Observation Assignment

Take a look at the eight communication sins and pick out the one that irritates you most. Count how many times you hear someone else use that expression today. Imagine how much more powerful each speaker would be without all those lame expressions.

CHAPTER 7

Perfecting Your Elevator Pitch: How to Wow Them in Just Three Floors

AFTER THE LESSONS OF THE LAST SIX CHAPTERS, you are now ready to put all of your new knowledge to work for you. The most likely place to start is the euphemistic "elevator pitch."

Your elevator pitch is a critical weapon in your professional revenue-generating arsenal. It's your audition for professional attention, your calculated attempt to be noticed and to matter to others. The skills to develop a strong elevator pitch will serve you well, forever. It's a set of skills most business people don't fully understand, but covet. It's the rare ability to capture the interest and imagination of someone you have just met—in about the time it would take both of you to enter an elevator, travel down to the lobby level, and then cross the office building foyer together before saying good-bye and heading in separate directions.

That's why they (you know "them") call this an elevator pitch, even though it has nothing to do with multiple-story buildings. Great communicators, those who connect quickly and strongly with others all the time, know how to communicate the essence of their message or presentation—succinctly and in a memorable way—whether or not there's an elevator in sight. Once we pump up your elevator pitch muscle, you'll flex it all the time: at industry conferences, at community networking meetings, on soccer or Little League fields, or at the board meetings at church.

Soon you'll be looking for opportunities to make a positive impact on others. And you'll do so, without stopping to think whether those listening to you will ever buy anything from you. This is what separates the "elevator pitch studs" from the large pack of ninety-pound-weakling communicators.

Elevator pitch superstars are always using their communication muscles, five to ten times a day or more. They don't worry about whether it's the right time or the right person for their pitch. They love what they do and they actively look for opportunities to share that joy with others. That means they'll work just as hard to make a connection with the cashier at the convenience store or the CEO of a large company at a Chamber of Commerce meeting.

The more you use your strong elevator pitch, the better it will get, and the more happiness and professional success it will bring you. The result is that your polished, dynamic elevator pitch can make an immediate difference. You will stop hearing the dismissive "Well, I certainly have enjoyed meeting you," and instead hear much more powerful words from your new acquaintance, magical words like:

"Wow, I need to know more about what you do."

"When can we get together for a cup of coffee to go over this?"

"Can I have your card?"

Even if the response is not that immediate or direct, you have made a powerful impression, and your listeners may be saying to themselves:

"Wow, we need someone like that to help our company."

"What great ideas and enthusiasm."

"I need to remember this."

"I need to tell others back at the office about this."

There's good incentive to devote the time it takes to create a winning elevator pitch. It the best marking tool, best sales tool, and best branding tool for you and your company. It's you in the flesh—all bright eyes and flashing smile—as you talk about what you do. In the elevator or at the kid's gymnastics meet, your "in-person" pitch is always more powerful than the best magazine ad, the most creative billboard, or the most clever broadcast spot. When you're breathing the same air they are, you can't be missed or glossed over. When you are right next to them, in the real or imagined elevator, you are difficult to ignore (although unfortunately, not impossible). At that moment, *you* are the ad campaign, *you* are the brochure and the business card, *you* are the brand, and *you* are the value proposition.

The elevator pitch scenario opens up a wide horizon for you. When someone turns, makes eye contact, and says, "Well, tell me about your company," you are now on stage with a waiting audience, and you had better be ready with your lines. It's the elevator pitch moment, and you need to rise to the occasion and take advantage of this tremendous opportunity: an in-person, eye-to-eye chance to connect with someone else. This is the reason our elevator pitch workout will now go into high gear.

What's Wrong with Your Current Pitch?

Chances are you are saying something right now that sounds perfectly reasonable to you, and yet at the same time is bland and not helpful. The problem with most elevator pitches is that they don't help the speaker. It all goes back to the "Mommy-and-

Daddy"-voice issue: Your elevator pitch will not be memorable just because it comes from you! It has to create a connection.

Many professionals, including very successful ones, fool themselves by believing their elevator pitches are strong because they contain:

- Accurate information

- Correct corporate titles

- Established industry jargon

- Accepted yet overused "business-speak"

You aren't helping yourself with these words and phrases, even though they may bounce off your lips with a confident cadence. The lessons of Chapter 5 taught us that industry jargon and MBA-wannabe speak do not create connections, no matter how accurate they are. Instead they make for an inconsequential elevator ride for everyone in listening distance.

Does your current elevator pitch include marketing slogans, mission statements, vision statements, and tag lines? Such bold statements work well in annual reports and advertisements, but they instantly weaken as they come out of your mouth. You are fooling yourself if you believe a slogan alone will make you credible, powerful, or interesting. If all you can do is parrot slogans and tag lines, you will sound like a mindless automaton, unwilling to work hard enough to demonstrate how valuable you and your organization really are.

Here's the reason for my irritation. The slogan-tag line-mission-vision route has you simply mouthing some words that cost your company hundreds of billable hours with an ad agency or strategic planning firm. It's not you in the elevator, it's just the high-priced ad agency guys speaking through your zombie-like human vessel.

Now, one final blow to your current elevator pitch. Numbers and geography are its enemies as well. They are so easy to spout, and yet so totally ineffective. Nobody ever responds to numbers and geography with the words, "Wow, let me get this straight, you've got 423 employees in six district offices across four different western states? Man! I've got to have your business card. This is indeed my lucky day. That's just the type of firm I'm looking for. Thank God you ran all those numbers by me."

The lame elevator pitches, the ones filled with titles, jargon, catch phrases, numbers, and geography all share the same fatal DNA. They are all weak because they are easy. They require little or no effort on your part. They are ineffective because they are not customized for you, your job, and your elevator ride. As long as you use them, you are not saying anything worth listening to. That will now change, however, as we'll go through the steps of building your great elevator pitch and getting you all pumped up!

Great elevator pitches are not two sentences long. Short is not good. It's lazy and ineffective. Great elevator pitches run to five sentences or even longer. As long as your elevator pitch is sound, well thought out, and compelling, your listeners will give you the length of time and attention you deserve. If your primary goal is brevity, you'll fail, because you'll fall back on your company slogans. You've got to say enough to be interesting, but not say so much that you're taking advantage of their patience. It's a fine line. You can walk it, successfully.

Great elevator pitches are memorable, vivid, and unique to your voice and the way you talk. That means there's work ahead for you. It's worth it. As you develop your elevator pitch, you'll build your confidence in your company and in yourself.

How to Build Your Pitch Step by Step

There's a cadence and a beat to every good elevator pitch. It's not just smooth and easy to understand, but it's also filled with impact and individuality. A good elevator pitch always impresses the listener with its intensity. Strong elevator pitches all follow the same protocol and steps, yet no two good ones sound alike because they are customized.

I'm going to give you the exact protocol and steps you'll need to follow for crafting your elevator pitch.

Step #1: Describe Your Business Using Non-Jargon Words

The first words that come out of your mouth in your elevator pitch should be a brief and memorable description of your business. Here comes the hard part: I'm going to ask that your description *exclude* all industry jargon. Industry jargon, especially technically accurate jargon, destroys your ability to be compelling and unique. All it does is make you ordinary and easily forgettable.

This "jargon disinfection" is going to be tough, as it is for all of the participants in my workshops. My guess is that almost every description of your business you are now offering (proudly, even) is accurate, but filled with words and phrases that rarely spark the slightest bit of recognition or interest with others, including your potential customers. Those in your industry will understand what you are saying, but because you are relying on jargon they will not take notice. You're just another guy in the industry.

Work hard to speak plainly and without jargon with that first sentence, and you will have them listening to you.

Step #2: Focus on Your Customers

Now that you've told the listener what your business is, immediately move to how you serve your customers. Describe specifically what you do for your clients, in plain and distinct language. Avoid vague, overused, self-congratulatory maxims like the following, which trigger an immediate snort of sarcasm from facetious souls like me:

- "We solve our client's problems."

- "We form a partnership with our clients."

- "Our clients have come to rely on our unparalleled level of service."

- "We're the go-to guys."

It all sounds familiar and safe. That's why these phrases are immediately meaningless. You're better off to rid yourself of these decrepit chestnuts and replace them with something more original. If you want to describe what you do for your clients, focus on the exact reason they pay you. If you find it unprofessional to mention your fee in describing your business, get over it. No one else will find your concentration on how you earn your money distasteful, especially not your clients. Every time they receive a bill from you, they think about the money they pay you and why it's a good investment. Try saying:

"Our clients:

- "hire us because we . . ."

- "invest in us because we . . ."

- "turn to us because we. . . ."

and then describe the specific service or product you provide for them. Try to describe precisely why they make the investment in you, not vaguely why they hire you (that is, no mention of "partnership" or being the "go-to guys") but specifically why they pay you, using direct and easy to understand language. And remember to do so without using jargon. This is your first breakthrough step in creating a vibrant and memorable elevator pitch.

Step #3: Focus on Overcoming Challenges Your Clients Are Facing

Here's where you can really shine. After you've described your business and talked about why your clients hire you, launch into a single, highly specific issue or problem with which you helped a single customer. "Oh no!" I hear you whine, "I can't boil everything we do down to one customer issue. That way they'll never know everything we can do." You're right and now I'm going to let you in on another nasty and deflating secret.

Nobody riding in the elevator with you wants to know everything your company does! They barely want to listen to you, but they have to because they're trapped. They're hoping you will be somewhat interesting, but they won't count on it because they've been bored to death so many times before. You can change all that and make their day by sharing a single vibrant story about how you helped a single customer, not everything you do to help all clients.

The movie *Titanic* was about Jack and Rose, not about all 1,700 on board who wished they'd waited for the next ship heading for New York. *The Godfather* was about Don and Michael Corleone, not the entire Mafia. *Dumb and Dumber* was about two idiots, not every idiot. *Animal House* was about the brothers in Delta House at Faber College, not about the fraternity system. These classic films illustrate that the more specific you are, the more compelling you are. You need to paint a specific picture of a single problem you helped tackle for a single client.

Step #4: Focus on a Happy Customer Ending

Finish with a flourish and make sure your story has a happy ending for the customer. When you describe a single problem or issue that your product or service resolved for a client, you are telling your listener that you are worth the investment others make in you. You're communicating in a memorable way without sounding lame or shallow. The successful solving of a customer issue or problem gives you instant credibility, which you can never hope to achieve by simply reciting marketing slogans.

Two Examples: One Lousy and One Good

Now let's take a look at some examples. I want to dissect two types of elevator pitches for the same company. One is the kind of bland bromide we are all used to hearing. The second example is what I hope you'll aspire to sound like.

The first example is ordinary, inoffensive, and accurate—but not helpful. I didn't have to rack my brain to come up with this, since I hear these types of introductions all the time.

The second example is the opposite: It is direct, uplifting, and easy to understand. Best of all, it's likely to deliver on the ultimate goal: People who hear it will want to hear more about this company. While it may sound informal to the ear, it has a punch and verbal acceleration that the bland MBA-speak pitch lacks. Let's take a look at both examples, sentence by sentence.

Pitch #1: Boring and Average Elevator Pitch

"I'm a partner in a large regional CPA firm. What sets our practice apart is our commitment to the highest standards of client service. We go beyond the balance sheets and income statements to help you understand the real drivers in your business and how you can maximize them. We have substantial expertise in both the audit and tax sides of our business."

And now let's take a closer look at each sentence:

• *"I'm a partner in a large regional CPA firm."*
On the surface this description appears merely innocuous

and bland, but on closer examination it reeks of insecurity and self-doubt. There's no reason for you to lead with the boast that you have successfully billed enough hours in your firm for the other guys (men and women) to cough up a partner position to you. No one you meet for the first time is curious about your title or position in your corporate pecking order, unless it's "President" or "Founder"—both of which can create interest and connection as long as you have more than five or six employees.

That fact that you have to mention your firm is a "large regional" raises far more questions than it answers. Why don't you work for a national firm? Maybe you couldn't hack the competition. Don't bring in geography or size in the first sentence. Those topics do not help you build a connection, even if you are the biggest with the most offices.

- *"What sets our practice apart is our commitment to the highest standards of client service."*

This sentence is the embodiment of the colloquial "blah, blah, blah." It's so ubiquitous that it has lost all meaning. But on the off chance that someone actually hears it, they will probably wonder about your sincerity. Any successful firm should be dedicated to the highest level of service. Would you ever admit you are dedicated to *moderate levels* of client service? Would you tell someone you have a *lukewarm commitment* to client service?

Telling anyone that you are dedicated to the highest client service is like proudly professing you are unfailingly faithful to your life partner. It should never have to be said.

- *"We go beyond the balance sheets and income statements to help you understand the real drivers in your business and how you can maximize them.*

This sentence starts out with real promise and then disintegrates. I like *"We go beyond the balance sheets and income statements."* The meaningless MBA-speak term "drivers" ruins the good start. If I'm in distribution, the drivers in my business are down at the loading dock, and they never hide from me. I don't have to pay someone in a fancy suit to find them. If I'm not clear about what "real drivers" are (are there "fake" drivers?), why would I want anybody to maximize them?

- *We have substantial expertise in both the audit and tax sides of our business.*

Telling someone in the third or fourth sentence what type of work your firm chases makes for an accurate but weak elevator pitch. It's vague and not helpful.

The last part of this sentence is a typical trap that many professionals fall into. They think that everyone they meet is knowledgeable and somehow interested in the way their particular industries are set up. I'm betting that most educated humans, even successful ones, don't know or care that accounting firms are sometimes divided into people who work on profit and loss statements, and others who work on tax returns—just the same way they don't know or care that some lawyers are litigators and others work on transactions, or that some general contractors work on residential buildings and others on office buildings.

For most people, an accountant is an accountant, a lawyer is a lawyer, and a contractor is a contractor. Your elevator pitch needs to be focused on delivering specifics about how you help your clients. That's the way to create a great connection without getting into meaningless industry labels.

Let's take another crack at this elevator pitch, this time following the four-step protocol that ensures elevator brilliance:

Pitch #2: Interesting and Distinctive Elevator Pitch

"We are accountants. We make sure you understand your financial statements. We want the process of billing your cus-

tomers and paying the bills from your vendors every month to wind up making you money, instead of giving you continual unprofitable headaches. We do lots of things, but here is a good example. Just last week we showed a client that they were mistakenly using two different vendors to buy the same thing for different offices, instead of getting the vendors to compete for one big order at a lower price. That change will save our client $100,000 during the next quarter alone."

I like the sound and beat of this. It's easy to understand and sounds confident without making baseless claims. It also makes a positive impression on the listener. The reason it succeeds is that it follows the elevator pitch protocol. Let's take a look at each sentence to discover how this speaker will make a great first impression every time with this introduction:

- *"We are accountants."*

This is a crisp and effective business label that is friendly and direct. It alone is not gripping, but it puts the listener at ease and creates the foundation for what is to follow. It should be delivered with a positive and strong tone. Many accountants sweat about introducing themselves because they know the popular culture dismissed their profession as one that attracts only boring people. Boring accountants are boring, but so are the boring people in any profession. I know a number of dynamic and brilliant accountants who are always a delight to connect with. You can change the misconception of the people you are meeting for the first time immediately, by stating you are proud of what you do and then launching into the rest of your pitch.

- *"We make sure you understand your financial statements. We want the process of billing your customers and paying the bills from your vendors every month to wind up making you money, instead of giving you continual unprofitable headaches."*

This is a winning elevator-pitch second sentence. It focuses on the client, and gives a powerful reason as to why the client hires the speaker. The speaker has made a jargon-filled technical profession easy and simple to understand.

- *"We do lots of things, but here is a good example. Just last week we showed a client that they were mistakenly using two different vendors to buy the same thing for different offices, instead of getting the vendors to compete for one big order at a lower price."*

This is a highly focused story of solving a problem for a client. It's quick and easy to understand, which is a blessing for everyone in the elevator. This is an area where most elevator pitches break down. They either never include a story, or the one they include is too detailed and boring. When you prepare your own story, editing and honing it over and over again will help you transform it from ordinary to great.

- *"That change will save our client $100,000 during the next quarter alone."*

This is a nice little close for a dynamic elevator pitch. The story works great with the punch line being any dollar amount—$100,000 or $1 million, it doesn't matter. It's a story about saving the client money through creativity and innovation, which is always a good story.

One Size Does Not Fit All

Not every pitch is right for every elevator. That's why you need more than one. Bummer, I know, but you can do it. Work hard to create five distinct elevator pitches. It's a reasonable goal. You can do it. Keep that opening sentence the same, but use five different stories of success to illustrate five different reasons customers pay you money. That way you'll be ready for any elevator, or any meeting, with confidence and cool.

You can do this. It is not intellectually challenging like quantum physics, Shakespeare, and that crazy iambic pentameter, or even Sudoku. All you need to do is follow the plan and have the burning desire to stop being ordinary.

Observation Assignment

Quietly critique the next elevator pitches you hear. Look to catch the lame industry jargon, meaningless numbers, and mission statements. Maybe you'll be lucky and hear a good one, one that has a strong opening, a quick customer story, and a happy ending. Watch how others react to this little gem, and realize it's worth all the prep time.

CHAPTER 8

How to Enhance Your Connections with Meaningful Praise and Helpful Criticism

IT'S ONLY NATURAL TO THINK that delivering a complimentary comment is an easy, effective way to create some positive karma in any conversation. It makes sense: Say something nice and you've upped the warmth in the room. Great communicators know it's not easy at all, and that delivering a compliment in the wrong way creates bad vibes that are hard to overcome. When you have "It," you only deliver compliments that are well thought-out and executed with care that will help you build strong connections.

In the same way, many of us look forward to having to deliver criticism with the same kind of enthusiasm we save for a colonoscopy. But that's not the way strong communicators look at the process of delivering criticism. They know it is a necessary part of the equation to build and maintain great connections with coworkers and family. When you have "It" you won't dread tough conversations. You'll know they are important and the key to making an impact and being memorable.

In this chapter we are going to break down both praise and criticism, examining the correct method of delivering both, so that you will not only maintain but increase your connections with others. Your new compliments and criticisms will not guarantee instant success in every scenario. But you will significantly increase your odds at having the one you compliment respond, "Thank you, that means a lot to me," and the one you criticize say, "I understand what you want me to do and I am going to start working on it now." Each of those is a win for your connections.

Couldn't Uncle Fred Have Stayed Home This Year?

We all have that irritating uncle who pushes back from the table after a holiday meal, and proclaims magnanimously, "Well, that was just great. Everything was really, really delicious. Of course, it always is. I just wouldn't expect anything else."

The host or hostess who has prepared the meal will smile wanly and murmur, "Thanks a lot," while really starting to fry inside and voicing the inner condemnation, "Yeah, thanks a lot for patronizing me and minimizing the last eleven hours of work I just went through!"

The full-of-it Uncle Fred shows us that delivering praise is dicey and dangerous, quickly murdering every bit of good karma in the room. "Hey, I was just being nice," your uncle would defend himself, if you ever called him on his irritating ways. "What's so wrong with that?" he would question, as if he were the greatest uncle in the world. What's wrong is that he phoned in the compliment. He didn't work hard enough. In fact, he didn't work at all at making you feel good; he was just patting himself on the back about being so smart as to anticipate your culinary excellence.

Don't mistake this for even a backhanded compliment; that at least takes a wry sense of imagination. This is a patronizing compliment, which is worse than no compliment at all. That's right: If you ever have the urge to use the expression, "Well, I just wouldn't expect anything less," just put a pillow over your mouth.

The road to communication hell is paved with those who will tell you they are just trying to be nice and encouraging. These vague and lackluster praisers, who believe they are wonderfully well-intentioned, would improve their lot if they worked more diligently at the protocol of actually saying something nice and complimentary.

Just like everything else that happens when you open your mouth to engage others, delivering effective and nurturing praise is a lot harder than it looks. Unless you construct a compliment properly, it will hurt you instead of helping you as you strive to connect with others. If you don't play by the compliment rules, you will sound insensitive, insincere, irritating, and boorish—*all at the same time.*

"How can that happen," some might whine, "when all I wanted to do was show someone else I appreciate their efforts?" A great communicator will counter that you didn't put forth the effort necessary to achieve your goal. Instead, you listened to the "Mommy and Daddy" voice telling you your compliments are wonderful just because, well, they come from you. Keep ignoring that voice. It's not helping you.

Delivering a compliment that works takes diligence and thoughtfulness. Just examine your own experience. We've all felt that sting of insincere compliments that left us resentful and distrustful of that relative, coworker, customer, supplier, or friend. When you decide to deliver a compliment, it's not a slam dunk, open-net goal, two-foot put, or what every tired sports metaphor you want to use. It's a challenge and there's no way around it.

The More Specific the Praise, the More Powerful the Connection

When you have "It," you know that delivering praise is always a process of entering a social minefield, where things can blow up quickly, sometimes even without your being aware of it. If you haven't made your praise specific nor used your picture-painting skills, you can hurt yourself more than help yourself. Let's take a look now at where the hidden bombs are in a number of different professional and personal situations.

Evaluating the Marketing Report

The Compliment Scenario: You want to praise a peer at work for their recent marketing report.

- *The Lousy Compliment:* "Hey, Barry, you did a pretty good job on the marketing report. You definitely brought up some good points. Keep up the good work!"

- *The Average Compliment:* "Hey, Barry, you did a good job on the marketing report. You brought up good points."

- *The Effective Compliment:* "Hey Barry, you did a good job on the marketing report. The third-quarter demographic stuff on the northeast region helped everyone focus on where the money is for us. I saw Gail was very impressed with your analysis of the competition from the offshore guys as well. I'm looking forward to your next go 'round.

Analysis:

The Lousy Compliment demonstrates how qualifiers and modifiers kill connections. "Pretty good" and "some" sound harmless, but because they qualify "good," this compliment will have Barry saying to himself, "What the heck to you mean 'pretty good.' I worked my tail off on every single item. They were all great points, down to the last one, and not just 'some' of them as you said. Thanks for nothing." If your compliment has Barry thinking this, you would have been better off talking to him about the weather. Finally, since you are a peer of Barry's and not his boss, it's a bad idea to tell him to keep up the good work. It's not your purview, and it only increases the level of resentment he's already experiencing because of your weak praise.

The Average Compliment is better than the lousy one, simply because it eliminates the qualifiers. This is an innocuous, nonconnective compliment. It doesn't hurt, but it doesn't help either.

The Effective Compliment works because it is specific, and it shows Barry that you understand how much work he did. Notice that the word "good" stays put. Effective compliments rarely rely on effusive words. If you told Barry his report was "stupendous," "awe inspiring," or "truly remarkable," he'd wonder how much money you needed to borrow. So "good" works well, and takes on more significance by the references to markets and competition. Barry knows you heard what he was saying, and that is high praise. The reference to Gail is a great touch because it shows Barry that others liked the report as well. Finally, saying you look forward to his next report is a great, nonpatronizing way to end the short conversation.

Complimenting a Client

The Compliment Scenario: You want to praise a prospective client for their recent success.

- *The Lousy Compliment:* "I'm really happy to meet with you today, because you guys are going through the roof with your sales. I mean you're riding a real rocket here. You must be delighted and tickled pink with your success."

- *The Average Compliment:* "I'm happy to be here today because your sales growth is impressive. This has got to be a good time for you."

- *The Effective Compliment:* "I read in the business journal that you've just signed a new contract with that company from Taiwan. And that follows several other new contracts I've read about as well. This must be an exciting time for you and provides lots of challenges for your whole team."

Analysis:

The Lousy Compliment is used by lots of sales professionals, who start their meetings with successful prospects like this. The sales guy gets off on the wrong foot in many ways. I ask all sales teams I coach to never start off a meeting by telling the prospect they are happy to meet with them. The prospect is not complimented by this. You are meeting with the prospect because you want their business, the order, their money. They know that. There's no reason to tell them you're happy or delighted to see them. It will not make their day. The diatribe about "riding a rocket" is silly and patronizing. Successful leaders have to deal with this type of disingenuous flattery all the time. These people are used to sizing up sycophants quickly, and the "through the roof" comments you have just made put you right on the list. Fifteen seconds into the meeting your lousy compliments have you worse off than you were before you stepped in the door.

The Average Compliment eliminates the "full of it" phrases featured in the lousy compliment. The result is a drab and inconsequential opening to the meeting. It's also a typical start.

The Effective Compliment works because it demonstrates to the prospect that you've already done your homework about the company. That is high praise, without a single blatantly complimentary remark. You think so highly of them as a potential prospect that you've been following their successes and can speak about them specifically. All sales meetings should start like this. It's a great way to get the attention of the prospect and let them know that you are a serious and hard-working potential vendor for them. Finally, the last line about challenges shows you have strong business acumen. Increased sales, especially rapidly increasing sales, always brings lots of problems. The effective compliment shows that you understand they have a full plate, and demonstrates you are grateful for their time without the pandering, "I know you're a very busy person. Thanks for working me in."

Getting Ready for the Party

The Compliment Scenario: You want to compliment your spouse as you prepare to leave for a party.

- *The Lousy Compliment:* "Well, what can I say? Once again you look stunning. You'll be the prettiest woman there."

- *The Average Compliment:* "You look great."

- *The Effective Compliment:* "You look great. The blouse and the earrings go great together. I don't think I have ever seen you wear that combination before. It really works."

Analysis:

Great communicators do not say "What can I say?" because they know they must work harder and say something, anything, that is more descriptive than the meaningless, self-congratulatory Socratic question. "Once again" makes it sound as if it's easy to look great, which it is not, neither for women nor for men. The spouse wants to know how she looks right now, not compared with the past. I'm going to go out on a limb and say that most mature women or men don't have it as their goal to be the "prettiest" or "handsomest" in the room, so this bit of praise is at best meaningless, and at worst, gratuitous.

The Average Compliment is simple, but even if true to the heart, it lacks punch because it is so brief and lacking in substance.

The Effective Compliment works on a number of different

levels. It's not over the top, because it starts with the straightforward, "You look great." Then follows the description of the specifics of the earrings and the blouse, which shows you really are paying attention. The final comment that this is a new combination is very helpful even if you may be wrong. It demonstrates the understanding of the effort that went into putting together the elements of the outfit. It's real, effective praise not only because it's sincere, but because it's specific.

* * * * * *

Now that we've seen how to build a great connection by delivering a proper compliment, let's briefly revisit Uncle Fred and show him doing the right thing. If that pompous uncle were to read this chapter, he'd push back from the table and say, "Every thing was delicious and flavorful. I especially enjoyed those green beans. They were so bright and colorful . . . sweet and crunchy with every bite. Mine never turn out that way! I can tell you worked hard on them, and everything else you put in front of us. It's an honor to be at your table."

As the host or hostess, you beam and make sure this now-redeemed Uncle Fred gets the first serving of dessert. The compliment was meaningful, respectful, and specific. It achieved its intended purpose. You're now thinking that all those hours in the kitchen were worth it, and you're pleased that everyone is together and happy because of your diligence.

Accepting a Compliment Also Takes Skill

Not only can you spoil your connection efforts by delivering a weak compliment, you can do the same by not accepting a compliment in the right way.

Here's an all-too-familiar dialogue featuring a poorly accepted compliment:

Phil: "Hey Joe, great job on the Landings Project. Everything was on time, despite the quarter-end crunch, and the client was just delighted with all the little touches you added at the last minute. You made us all look great."

Joe: *"Well, aw, shucks . . . it really wasn't much of anything."*

Phil: "What are you talking about? We all sat back and marveled as you pulled the rabbit out of the hat day after day. It took a lot of extra work, and we all appreciate it."

Joe: *"Gee, I don't know about that. Just doing my job, that's all."*

Phil: "Well, I'm not going to argue with you, but it was still a great job."

Joe's professed modesty and repeated deflection of the compliment can seriously hurt his relationship with Phil. There is no value in Joe's disagreeing with Phil, especially when Phil is working hard to deliver a sincere and well-thought-out comment. You should never disagree with someone trying to be kind and decent by paying you a compliment. The "aw-shucks" bit is a turnoff because Joe winds up questioning the accuracy of Phil's observations or the value of his opinion.

Here's a successful connection in the same scenario:

Phil: "Hey Joe, great job on the Landings Project. Everything was on time, despite the quarter-end crunch, and the client was just delighted with all the little touches you added at the last minute. You made us all look great."

Joe: *"Thanks, Phil. That means a lot to me. The project was a lot of work, but I am also pleased with the way it turned out. The whole division worked hard to make it happen, especially Jorge and Julia."*

Phil: "Really, I didn't know they were involved. I'll have to make sure I say something to them."

Joe: "*I know they'd love the pat on the back.*"

Phil: "I'll do it today. Thanks again."

This response makes Joe look like the star that he is. First of all, he acknowledged and accepted Phil's compliment, creating a nice connection. Next, he showed real, not false, modesty by turning attention to other members of the team. This quick little bit of compliment acceptance does wonders for Joe in a short exchange. It also beats the heck out of arguing with Phil, who is working hard to build a connection as well.

Delivering Criticism Effectively

It's a curious feeling for Sharon. Her mood is good and she's wondering how on earth that's possible. She just walked out of the boss's office after her annual review, which, as it turned out, was not altogether positive. He did point out six or seven troubling things she needs to work on to succeed in the coming year. But despite that, Sharon doesn't feel bad at all. In fact, she's upbeat and energized, ready to get back to her desk and make the magic happen in her department. The boss gave her specific items to work on, and a tight time frame for cleaning up her act in those areas.

But during the whole review process, she never felt inferior, incompetent, or resentful. She found herself actually enjoying hearing the bad along with the good. She also realized she listened carefully to her boss throughout the entire hour.

"Boy," Sharon thinks, "it never works that way when I have to review the people who report to me." Her direct reports become surly and sullen for days and weeks afterward, even though she had only pointed out what should have been obvious. On top of that, her employees never show very much improvement. Were they even listening? Sharon wants to know what her boss knows that she doesn't.

Everyone remembers the heart-felt lessons of a boss who was tough but fair, helping us develop strong skills in the process. Delivering a rave review or good news is pleasant and simple to accomplish. Learning how to deliver criticism, however, is much more difficult.

And criticism is the right word. No one respects someone who is endlessly agreeable. There are times when you have to criticize an idea, a plan, or someone's actions. When you have "It," you know that taking a stand, even saying "this is not a good idea," is key to having others listen and pay attention to you.

In the following scenarios we won't judge criticism on whether it is "constructive" or "nonthreatening." Great communicators don't worry about labels, because they know powerful, connective criticisms are always "constructive" and "nonthreatening." They are far more concerned about making sure that criticisms are effective and build connections.

Let's take a look at three scenarios—two in the workplaces and one at home—where the goal is to deliver criticism in the hopes of changing future behavior or actions. The scenarios won't involve any extenuating circumstances. Sometimes there just aren't any: the idea was bad, the guy was late today, or your partner let you down. I'm sure you'll hear lots of words and expressions that you and others around you have used.

Criticizing with Sarcasm

Criticism Scenario: Conference room, criticizing a colleague's idea to raise prices of certain items.

- *Weak Criticism:* "I can't believe this is even on the table. Why don't we just hand our customers over to our competitors on a silver platter? If we follow your plans we'll be delivering customers right to their doorsteps, with everything except a bow. On top of that I'll never see another commission dollar because I'll never make a sale. This is a horrible idea. Other than that I really like it."

- *Effective Criticism:* "I vote against raising our prices and here's why: You are right. Some of our customers won't mind the increase and we'll create some more margin for us. This won't work across the board, though. I predict most of our customers won't stand for it. Instead, they'll start looking elsewhere to buy what they buy from us. That means we'll wind up losing money plus the customers we worked so hard over the years to get into our camp. We do need to raise our margins, but we have to look at some other way to get there.

Analysis:

The Weak Criticism is filled with sarcasm, which destroys instead of builds connections. Sarcasm stings and creates far greater damage than a direct, harsh statement like, "I think this is a really lousy idea." Great communicators measure their use of sarcasm wisely, always evaluating whether the wit is worth the sting of comment. The final reference to commission is self-serving, even though it's probably true. The compensation structure is not what the discussion is about, and bringing it up only weakens the criticism.

The Effective Criticism focuses entirely on the effect of the price increase on the company's relationships with the customers. The opening line is direct, followed by a sincere concession that that plan will have a measure of initial success. This is a far more connective way of setting the stage for your next remarks than saying, "I see where you are going with this, and I certainly agree to a certain extent." That's patronizing and weak. It's better to just give your colleague his due, and then move on, with the clear, direct criticism, "Your plan will give us some gains, but they will be overshadowed by our losses." This is what "It" is all about: direct, strong, respectful communication, regardless of agreement or disagreement.

Criticizing with an Apology

Criticism Scenario: your office, criticizing the shipping clerk for showing up to work late.

- *Weak Criticism:* "Well, you know how much we think of you around here, so I really hate to mention this to you. But we really need you in here at 8 A.M. every day, and several days this week you didn't make it in until about 8:30. So, could you please try to make it here at 8 every day?"

- *Effective Criticism:* "I need to talk to you about your being late several days this week. We need you in here at 8 A.M. every day. When you don't show up until 8:30, it throws everyone off: not only the people in shipping, but the shop floor, customer service, and even accounting. So your work day starts at 8, and that's when I look forward to seeing you from now on.

Analysis:

Starting a criticism with an apology is no way to get someone to change their behavior and to get them to pay attention to you. It only makes them wonder why if you "think so much" of them, and that you really "hate to bring it up," then why bother with this trivial item. Either this is worth talking about or not. Further, this should not be a request. Work starts at 8, and punctuality is what is expected. There is no reason to mildly plead or to add "please." Also, notice how the qualifier "really" weakens every sentence it touches.

The Effective Criticism is direct, strong, and complete. There are no hand-wringing explanations about how difficult this conversation is. The great communicator knows that one thing has nothing to do with the other. This shipping clerk may be a valuable employee, but that does not change the fact he is hurting the company if he continues to be late for work. This is respectful communication because it tells the shipping clerk he is valuable by painting a picture of his value to the organization.

Criticizing with Questions

The Criticism Scenario: The kitchen table, criticizing your spouse for not checking the take-home order before leaving the restaurant.

- *The Weak Criticism:* "Hey, there's no extra salsa in the bag. Where is it? Didn't you check the order before you left the restaurant? Where is the extra salsa? You know I like the way they make it there."

- *The Effective Criticism:* "Hey, there's no extra salsa in the bag. I'm bummed out. I love the way they cut the tomatoes and add that extra cilantro. Could you check the bag before you leave the restaurant next time? I'll put out the plates. Let's eat."

Analysis:

The Weak Criticism is combative and nasty because the answers are obvious, making the whole communication facetious. The answer to the first question is that the extra salsa is back at the restaurant, and everybody knows it. The answer to the second question is even more obvious: If the partner had checked the order, the extra salsa would be in the bag, so no, she did not check the order. So this criticism is nothing more than a harangue. If the goal is to chastise, this works well. If the goal is to build a connection to improve the environment (and get the salsa next time, as well as getting through the evening without a fight), this is a huge failure.

The Effective Criticism is direct, simple, and quick. It even adds a little picture of why that salsa is worth all this discussion. Then it's over. Great communicators make their point, criticize a specific action or idea, ask for a more positive action next time, and then move on.

If You Can Dish It Out, You'd Better Know How to Take It

When you are on the receiving end of a fair and effective bit of communication, you should be happy, not defensive. It means the other person in the room wants a strong connection with you and is willing to put in the work necessary to get there with you. It also means you never have to roll over: You could continue to fight for your price increase, pull up the master schedule that has you working from 8:30 to 5:30 this week, or explain that the restaurant ran out of extra salsa just when you were picking up the order.

If You Are Wrong, Admit It

Some of the greatest connections are built with the words, "You are right, I am wrong. I am sorry." As long are you are sincere and not manipulative, sarcastic, or just saying the words to get out of the meeting in one piece, you have built a strong connection.

No excuses. The heartfelt words, "You are right, I am wrong, I am sorry" are a magical communication elixir that so few are willing to take a sip of. It creates instant warmth, relief, and connection in the room. Please take full advantage of the powerful admission of wrong. Weak communicators waste millions of brain calories trying to avoid admitting they're wrong. It's a waste of time. When you have "It," it will be easy to admit you're wrong. And you know you'll be better off for it.

Observation Assignment

Keep track of when you are being complimented or criticized by others, even slightly. Watch for it in your colleagues at work and from your family members at home. Make a quick evaluation answering these questions:

- Were they direct?
- Were they apologetic?
- Did I feel they were sincere?
- Did I feel the sting of sarcasm?
- Did I feel more or less connected to them after they delivered the compliment or criticism?
- Did I feel the criticism was reasonable?
- Did I feel the compliment was well thought-out or glib?
- Did the criticism have me realize I should change my behavior?

Now that you know what is effective and what is weak, you'll be tempted immediately to coach others on their complimenting and criticizing skills. Hold off for a while. We'll tackle that later in Chapter 11.

CHAPTER 9

How to Succeed at "Small Talk" (It's the Only Way to Get to "Big Talk")

IT'S DIFFICULT FOR JOSH to shake off the jealousy. After all, he's been sweating since the moment he left his keys with the valet and entered the hotel ballroom. He hates these cocktail hour, industry networking things. But Josh's boss says she's tired of being the only rainmaker in the department and he needs to get "out there." So here he is, "out there," juggling a plate of Swedish meatballs and a vodka and tonic, while forcing a smile and unsuccessfully trying to get into a business card exchange with the person next to him.

Suddenly, Josh sees a confident man who obviously likes this drill, given the look of his easy smile and the warm greetings he receives from others. "Well, I see a Mr. Schmoozer has entered the room," Josh says to himself. "Oh, oh, here he comes." The man walks right up to Josh and says, "Hi . . . say those meatballs look good, are they worth the calories I know are embedded inside each one?" Josh is taken slightly off guard by the forward yet friendly question, and before he knows it he's in a great conversation with the guy.

The fellow quickly demonstrates to Josh that he understands what Josh does and what his business issues are. More importantly, Josh understands the guy, what he does, and how competent he is. "Come to think of it," Josh wonders, "should I mention this meeting to my boss? Yeah, that's right; maybe we could subcontract some projects out to this guy. Sounds like he'd do a great job, take the pressure off us, and make us look really good. Great idea," Josh tells himself.

That's when the envy strikes light a bolt of lightning. "Wait a minute! How did this stranger just walk up to me, and ten minutes later I'm ready to give him a purchase order so he can send me a bill," Josh thinks. "What happened? I could never do that." Josh has just witnessed the work of a communications superstar, one who can make a strong, instant connection, and everyone is better off because of it.

The path to strong connections always starts small. It can build very quickly, but the first couple of connection steps must be brief and steady, so that everyone can establish their footing. And there are specific steps that will help you build quick connections with people you meet for the first time. The people who travel through every reception with ease and light up every conversation they enter know these steps and follow them every time. They don't dread or disdain small talk, just as they don't dread or disdain booting up a computer. It's just a step in the connection process.

Start your small talk with questions about kids, families, work, and hobbies, all of which are great foundation setters. Anything more intense will make the people you are hoping to connect with uncomfortable. No one wants to pursue a conversation with someone who says the first time they meet, "Hey, I'm very glad to meet you. I wanted to discuss my belief that the roots of terrorism date back to just after World War II, when we limited the Marshall Plan to Europe when it should have included the Middle East as well." It sure is "big talk," and perhaps an interesting topic to discuss, but it's too heavy, too abrupt, and just too weird of a conversation to launch into over the first beer or an early-morning Danish. "Creepy" is not a good adjective to have attached to your name when you're trying to build a connection.

Still, lots of people I know say they hate small talk, as if they wish that every conversation should be one erudite exchange on *PBS News* after another. "Small-talk haters" want an invigorating social connection to be handed to them on a gold platter, free and easy with no investment required. When that's not happening, they sniff that the world around them is just one never-ending, shallow episode of *Access Hollywood*.

If you have "It," you know that those who say they hate small talk just don't want to spend the time and energy needed to make a connection with new people they meet. They still believe the "Mommy and Daddy" voice that tells them they are far too brilliant to talk about anything they don't want to talk about at that moment. These small-talk haters are so convinced that the pedestrian conversations that make up most of real life are so meaningless that they are better off smugly keeping their mouths shut.

That type of haughtiness, combined with laziness and the dread of actually having to exert some effort in chatting with strangers—whether the people at the cocktail party, the woman sitting next to you on the plane, or the receptionist at your first appointment—causes the small-talk hater to miss out on a lot. Others will never listen to you if you can't consistently muster the energy and enthusiasm to listen to them. Those who have "It" use any small-talk situation to practice their connection-building skills in a risk-free environment. They look forward to succeeding at making small talk, knowing they never know when it will help them succeed.

This chapter shows you how to make small talk easy, and how it might lead to "big talk," if there is such a thing. Just as there is a story-telling protocol, there's a definite successful pattern to follow in making connections with people you meet for the first time in business, networking, or social situations. It can make you interesting in a hurry. Once you learn how to use the protocol, you can keep using it over and over again.

Let's go through the exercise of making thoughtful small talk that builds the connection necessary to get to big talk. I'll show you the art of asking detailed, friendly questions—the kind that others will quickly and instantly reciprocate.

Questions Are the Key

The art of making successful small talk is the skill of asking insightful questions. The questions are the spark that creates intimacy and the sharing of experiences, which quickly lead to new connections. Those who have "It" know that if they can ask four successful questions about the same topic in reasonable succession, they will make a connection.

The first question should be broad, the second one more focused, and the final question narrow. After asking three questions, offer up some information of your own, based on the responses you've been getting. This is your declaration that you are interested enough in making a connection to share something about yourself. Your declaration should end with a quick fourth question.

The goal of the declaration is to give the other person the opportunity to ask you a question to keep things rolling. If they ask a question based on your declaration, you are on your way to connecting. If not, get ready to move on or switch to another topic.

Topics That Work

Let's get to the topics that work. I favor, in order, the following topics as a compelling way to get to know someone at your next cocktail party:

1. Employment, Profession

2. Hometown

3. Hobbies, Activities

Forget Weather

If you go all the way to the gutter of small talk—the weather—you are sending signals that you may be borderline socially pathetic. Harsh, I know.

If you find yourself asking a question like, "Ready for this summer heat to be over?" you might as well hang a sign around your neck that reads, "I have no idea how you and I could ever find common ground, so I'm going to invest as little as possible. You see, I'm not talented enough to discuss anything else, and I'm really not interested in finding out much about you either." Besides, the question is inane because everyone knows the response.

You probably sensed this the last time you mimicked, "Hot 'nough for 'ya?" But until you picked up *The "It" Factor*, you didn't know any better. Now you do. So remember, except for some rare exceptions (disastrous hurricanes, record snow storms), weather is off limits.

Sports Are Almost As Bad

If you have to default to major league and college televised sports as your only means of making a small-talk connection, you are demonstrating a lack of confidence in your connection skills. Inquiring about sports may be easy, perhaps, but it's not powerful. If you are one of those people who watches *SportsCenter* on ESPN—both before midnight and then the repeat showing after midnight (you know who you are)—you should know you are in the minority. It's a fervid minority that no one is besmirching, but there are lots of other people out there who are addicted to business magazines, novels, the History Channel, or *The Sopranos*. Those who are not sports addicts usually wait a while before tipping their hands, and thus would never open a conversation with a new acquaintance by asking, "Jeez, can you believe how Tony is treating Carmella? He doesn't know what a great woman he has there. And he better stop putting so much faith in Christopher. I haven't trusted that kid since Season Four. What do you think?" Please pardon my personal obsession with *The Sopranos*. Even though I'd like to start my Monday morning conversations with these questions, I know they will not work.

The sports-question guys lose out because they take for granted everyone shares their passion. Some people will, others won't, but the sports question is a low-percentage way to make a connection. Not everybody loves sports, but everybody has a profession, a hobby, and a hometown. Better to use those, and see whether sports comes up naturally later in the discussion. As with the weather, there are exceptions, such as the Super Bowl, which most save cloistered monks watch or are at least aware of.

I know that some of you reading this are protesting loudly that the World Series, the NBA playoffs, the Final Four of March Madness, the BCS Championship, as well as the final rounds of the U.S. Open in tennis and golf are stirring events and always worthy of chit-chat. They are, but they are not the highest percentage shot at making a connection in two or three minutes. There's nowhere to go when the other guy says, "You know, I don't really follow golf." Thud goes the connection process.

Small Talk Cadence: Four Questions, One Declaration

Now that weather and sports are off limits, let's see how this formula plays out with examples from our approved list of topics.

Topic: Employment–Professional

Question 1: *"What do you do?"*

Response: "I'm an attorney at Smith, Wolfson and Hadad."

Question 2: *"What type of law do you practice?"*

Response: "I'm in real estate litigation."

Question 3: *"Are you in the middle of a trial right now?"*

Response: "No, but we have one set for next week. It's really crunch time, and I'm going to have to duck out of here early tonight."

Declarative Statement and Question 4: *"I know Sylvia Jenkins at Fleming and Davis . . . I think she's a litigator. Have you bumped in to her?"*

Response and Question: "I know Sylvia very well. We sit on the continuing education panel for the county bar association. She's great. How do you know Sylvia?"

Analysis: Four quick questions, and you've learned a lot. Your new friend has an upcoming trial that is demanding a lot of time, and you know someone in common. After you get done with discussing Sylvia, a normally social person may ask you some additional questions and the cadence of building a connection will start to quicken.

The first question—"What do you do?"—is the critical start to this process. You are declaring, "I am going to try to connect with you right now." It's a direct and fair question, and it's necessary to get going.

Thud Factor: Almost none. If someone is between jobs, they will usually share that with you, which opens up a whole new set of discussion items.

Topic: Home Town

Question 1: *"Where are you from?"*

Response: "Well, I grew up in the suburbs of Minneapolis. I went to Edina High School".

Question 2: *"Wow, how did you get down here?"*

Response: "Well, I met my wife at the University of Minnesota, and after graduation she got a great job offer with this software development company here in Atlanta. So we packed up, and I started to look for an architectural firm to sign on with."

Question 3: *"Do you miss Minnesota?"*

Response: "You know everyone asks if I'm glad to be here where it's so much warmer. I have to admit that I don't miss the winters, but I do miss my family and friends all the time. We go back twice a year."

Declarative Statement and Question 4: *"I went to a conference once in Brainerd, but it was in the summer, so I didn't get a real taste of the Minnesota winter. Have you been up there?"*

Response and Question: "You bet. My folks used to have a little cabin on a lake in Nisswa, which is right outside of Brainerd. They have some great resorts in Brainerd. Where did you stay when you were there?"

Analysis: This is a treasure trove of information. With the four questions and follow-ups we found out where he went to college, what his wife does, what he does, and where he vacations. These are all great connection points to pursue.

Thud Factor: Almost none. Everyone has a home town that they either think fondly of, or are glad not to be living in anymore.

Topic: Hobbies/Activities

Question 1: *"When you aren't practicing law, what do you do to relax?"*

Response: "About two years ago a friend invited me to a yoga class and I've been an addict ever since. I even bring my mat with me in my suitcase when I travel."

Question 2: *"Do you feel it gives you enough of a workout?"*

Response: "You know I've wondered the same thing when I watch the people in the yoga class at the gym. But I can tell you it's the best exercise program I've ever done."

Question 3: *"How often do you take yoga classes?"*

Response: "Only a couple of days a week. I still do cardio and free weights though. I like the balance."

Declarative Statement and Question: *"I'm finding that ever since I hit forty, I'm just not as flexible as I used to be. Touching my toes is a joke, I'm lucky to touch my knees. Would yoga help me with that?"*

Response and Question: "Yes, that's one of the huge benefits. Just try it once or twice. My bet is you're going to get into it very quickly. It's relaxing and strenuous at the same time."

Analysis: With this exchange, you've tapped into the other person's passion in a very specific way. It's a very quick connection builder. When you ask someone about a hobby or athletic activity, it's easy for them to share information with you, since most people like to spread the gospel of their passion. It doesn't matter that you don't participate in bass fishing, Pilates, golf, or clogging. You've shown an interest and they will want to talk about it. So much the better if they want to encourage you to consider taking up their passion. You don't have to, but you can always listen attentively to their pitch.

Thud Factor: Almost none, unless you bump into a member of a religious cult. Everybody likes to do something. They will talk about it when you prompt them through your four questions.

Wait Before Asking About the Spouse and Kids

If the other person mentions kids and/or spouse, follow up with questions. Most people not on the verge of a nasty breakup will respond favorably to questions about the spouse. And if you ask about the kids (how old are they, where do they go to school, what sports do they play) they will light up with intensity when they get a chance to talk about their activities and interests. There's a good chance some of those activities may overlap with what is going on in your household. But wait until they mention the spouse and the kids so you don't get caught in that uncomfortable moment for both of you when they mention they have no life partner or children. It's uncomfortable only because you asked. Follow up on the spouse and kids with questions, but only if they intersect the topics first.

You May Still Get Stonewalled

If you are doing your best and are getting no more than a grunt or two, just forget about it and move on. Your "It" factor skills do not guarantee success; they just better your chances. Perhaps the other person is having a bad day, or has sized you up and doesn't think you are worth the energy. Nothing beyond these topics we've gone through will convince them to engage. Go find someone worthy of your considerable talents.

They Too May Have "It"

You're going to start bumping into others who have the networking skills. When you recognize they have "It," just like you, it
will start to be fun quickly. Both of you will be asking questions,
sometimes right on top of each other. You'll chuckle and take
turns, realizing this is what networking is supposed to be like.
You'll connect quickly and win a new valuable addition to your
Outlooks contact list.

Warning: Give Everyone Their Due

Few episodes in life have us feeling more belittled or insulted
than being in a conversation with someone who is talking or
listening, but always looking over, above, and beyond us. And it
always delivers a direct message, "Well, I'm standing here with
you, but believe me, I know there's a better conversation in this
room somewhere. So I'm going to remain in your space for a
few minutes, but boy, as soon as I make eye contact with someone better than you, you are history. That's why even though you
and I are now talking, I am looking around to see if I can better
myself." These "look-pasters" are thoughtless and insecure, and
everyone who comes in contact with them knows it. It's so obnoxious, it's the one negative trait that even pure-of-heart non-
gossips will find themselves gossiping about. Of course, these
"look-pasters" could also just be self-centered, looking around to
make sure everyone is noticing that they're talking with Mr. Big.

So remember to stay in the conversation you're in without
demeaning the person you're talking to. Give them two minutes
of your time, even if you feel trapped by someone shopping a
resume or trying to sell you something you don't need. Be classy.
Give them their two minutes. Most importantly, keep looking at
them. After they've had their shot, touch their sleeve and say,
"I've enjoyed talking to you. I want to move on and say hello to

some other people." Then exchange cards, the ultimate show of respect. It's direct, it's fair, and you might just make someone's day. It's a waste of energy to constantly track the value of each possible connection. Stop worrying about it and connect as often as possible, and successful networking and social meetings will come your way.

As I've gotten older, I find I have less and less tolerance for "look-pasters," and I may even express my frustration by asking, "Look, if there is someone else you need to catch up with, please go ahead." The message is clear: If I'm so pedestrian, move on fast and stop insulting me with your loss of eye contact. This is usually followed by an apology and the attempt at a polite connection with me. I'm not suggesting that you take this confrontational approach often, because you might be creating moments of discomfort that won't be worth it for you. I pick my spots carefully when I use it.

What Josh Needs to Know

At the beginning of this chapter, Josh was amazed that he met someone who had connected with him instantly. Josh wondered how the guy was able to build rapport, establish his credentials, and even get Josh to give him a sizeable order, effortlessly and in a short period of time. After going through the small-talk protocol in this chapter, we now understand it was not effortless. But it was quick and pleasant. Let's take a look at how "the guy," whom we'll call Smith, was able to pull off this networking success, leaving Josh scratching his head:

Smith: *"Are those Swedish meatballs worth the calories I know are embedded in each one."*

Josh: "Well, they're kinda dry. I guess they've been out for a while. I'd go for something else if I were you."

Smith: *"Thanks for the advice. I will. Now that you've steered me in the right direction, please tell me what you do."*

Josh: "I work for Williamson and Associates . . . we're an IT outsourcing company."

Smith: *"Who are your customers?"*

Josh: "Mostly service and health-care firms. Both here and on the West Coast."

Smith: *"Tell me how your year is going. Are your numbers where you want them to be?"*

Josh: "Great! Way better than we expected. But that's given us some headaches. Our new volume has caused us lots of problems, especially in the accounting area. We're really struggling with our billing and are getting a lot of complaints from our customers."

Smith: *"We see that all the time in our business. Increased sales are a great thing, but it causes a different set of problems all their own. What are you doing to resolve the backlog in accounting?"*

Josh: "Going crazy mostly. It's very stressful. You said you see this all the time in your business. Tell me what you do."

Smith: *"I'm a partner in an outsource accounting and bookkeeping firm. We work with successful companies that grow fast and are overwhelmed by all the paperwork their new sales can generate."*

Josh: "Man, it sounds like we could use you! Let me tell you more about the jam we're in."

So it seems like Smith really lucked out this time, but that's not true. Smith uses this small-talk routine every time he jumps into a networking, small-talk situation. Sometimes it pays off big time, sometimes he just makes a new contact, and sometimes the other guy doesn't want to talk. Smith doesn't care. He knows that this is a good process, and he's going to keep following it.

Besides, he enjoys getting to know little and big things about others by asking a few key questions. Networking events are a joy for Smith.

His approach worked with Josh because he followed the protocol exactly: three questions, followed by a declaration and a fourth question. He resisted the temptation to whip out his business card immediately, the way so many professionals do when they are in networking situations. Hold on to your card until you make a connection. Then there is some value to the card and it will not wind up in the trash.

Josh will not just keep Smith's card, but he'll keep it so he can give Smith a call. Josh will look good to his boss, and Smith will get a new customer, all because Smith was willing to put the effort into small talk. The new contract with Josh's company proves that small talk leads to big talk.

Observation Assignment

Watch the pros in action and seek to learn from the best. At your next networking opportunity, seek out and listen in on some of the more lively conversations. Watch the ones who are powering these exchanges and count their probing questions. Take in what they sound like and how they craft their questions to promote new connections. Finally, try to see yourself in their role at your next event, where *you* will be asking the questions, sharing information, and taking home more business cards.

CHAPTER 10

How to Get Noticed at Meetings

CONFERENCE ROOM MEETINGS ARE NO FUN when you lack the ability to make fast and quick connections in these intense environments. This chapter will help you change all that. Realizing that you will be seen but rarely heard makes it tough to come to work every day. Knowing you will be outright ignored is just painful.

Meetings are a tremendous opportunity for you. They can be a low-risk, high-reward opportunity for you to showcase your intellect, hard work, and insight. But in line with the theme of this book, meetings take work. Those who make those great connections with everyone at meetings are working very hard before and during the meeting, and after they leave the conference room. They could leave everything to chance, maybe the way you do now, but they understand there is no reason to. When you have "It," you are happy to make the necessary effort, because you know it's worth it to your career.

The steps outlined in this chapter will give you the potential to shine in meetings, where corporate politics and egos are always bubbling underneath the surface of the topics at hand. Here we're not concerned with how to run a meeting, or how to deliver a successful presentation. That's for other chapters in other books. The goal of this chapter is to help you make an impact in meetings where you have been invited by others who need your intellect and your expertise. That impact will come from your new skill at connecting with a number of people at the same time.

So, let's set the ground rules for the type of meeting we're going to dissect, and find the spots for you to star in. We will concentrate on meetings that focus on implementing change in procedures, direction, or strategy. We'll focus on small but not intimate meetings: five to ten participants in a conference room.

Most meetings are not monumental exercises that cut to the core of organizational success or failure. Instead, most meetings are about small issues or opportunities that need to be flushed out and then addressed. But that doesn't mean your effective participation is not critical. If you can't demonstrate your value in these small meetings, you can forget about being invited to the ones where the big bosses decide major issues, such as making an acquisition or accepting a merge offer. You have to prove that you can bring a lot to the table, in every conference room meeting you attend.

Sample Meeting Scenarios

With that specific focus in mind, we'll discuss three meeting scenarios that focus on important but not earth-shaking issues.

Meeting Scenario #1: Winning Back the Small Business

Industry: Financial Services Company

Meeting Attendees: The marketing department of the western region

Meeting Issues: Your company has always served both the high net-worth customers and the average retail consumer customers very well. But in the last two years you've been losing the small-business owners to the competition. These middle customers are very good in terms of fees and long-term loyalty. The big bosses on the coast don't like to see this revenue or customer base going away.

Meeting Boss: Your boss, who is the head of marketing for the western region, is calling this meeting. She has taken on the responsibility for developing an action plan to win back the small-business owners. She wants this to be a prototype for the company.

Your Role: You implement all of the retail point of sale marketing campaigns. That means you're in charge of the design and production of signs, banners, and special promotions every month that catch the attention of the retail clients and keep them comfortable and loyal to your bank. This meeting has nothing to do with your expertise, but you were included on the e-mail invite list because the boss wants all ten people in the marketing department to attend.

Meeting Scenario #2: Handling Production Problems

Industry: Promotional Products Manufacturing and Distribution Firm

Meeting Attendees: The executive team

Meeting Issues: Your company has developed an expertise in imprinting imported desk clocks that customers use as gifts and leave-behinds. Your sales force keeps hitting home run after home run with some great national accounts, and the company can't keep up with demands.

Meeting Boss: Both the president and the owner want everyone's input on whether to start subcontracting out some of this work to competitors or to add a new production line.

Your Role: You are the assistant vice president of production. Your background is in industrial engineering, and you know exactly how much labor it takes to turn out every single specially imprinted clock the company sells. You have little understanding of marketing, sales, or why so many corporations buy these things.

Meeting Scenario #3: Winning Back the Client or Letting Go

Industry: Architecture and Design Firm

Meeting Attendees: The firm's partners and the design team

Meeting Issues: Your firm is in a quandary. In a company that has been a long-time corporate customer, a new vice president of facility development has just been appointed, and he is not a fan of your firm. He has let it be known that he prefers several of your competitors. You can either say good-bye to that nice but not critical piece of revenue, or try to win him over.

Meeting Boss: The partner in charge of the design team has called the meeting of the partners and everyone on the team.

Your Role: You are an architect in the group, several years out of school now. You've worked on a number of this customer's projects, but you have never been the lead contact.

* * * * * *

Now that we have our three scenarios, we're going to follow each one through the steps great communicators take to create a positive impact in each meeting they attend. These steps may appear plodding or unnecessary to you, but that's just the "Mommy and Daddy" voice whispering in your ear. Ignore it and go through these steps. Your confidence and your performance in meetings will improve.

Preparation

You need to prepare for every meeting you are asked to attend, if you want to create maximum impact. This prep time is worth it. You may not get a one-on-one with the boss except maybe once or twice a year. But if she can observe your insight and the results of your hard work in the conference room, you are helping your career.

Phase I: Your Questions

As you prepare for the meeting, you will have to do some investigating. This will involve a couple of conversations, where you will be asking questions. Here is what you need to find out:

- What is this meeting about?

- Who will be there?

- What can I prepare?

- What do I want to accomplish?

- What will be the follow-up?

These are not the exact questions you would ask, because they are too literal. They would be different for each scenario, as we will find out. But you need to find out the answers to these questions so that you can finish the next step of your preparations. You should direct your questions to the person who can give you new insight about the meeting, information that you don't already have. Pick someone high on the food chain whom you feel comfortable approaching. This could mean your boss, your boss' boss, or the person in the cubicle next to you who has some timely information. If you're not satisfied with the answers, try someone else.

Even if you think you already know the answers to these questions, it's still a good idea to ask them, because it's going to help you gain additional understanding of the political landscape. This is not to help you play politics, but rather to help you understand the politics. When you have "It," you know how important it is to make sure you are not needlessly stepping on toes. Mentioning something that is off limits can often bring a meeting to a screeching halt. Let's see how these questions play out and what information you can gain in each of our three scenarios.

Scenario #1: Winning Back the Small Business

You bump into your boss at the coffee machine and start gathering information.

You: *"Sally, are we going to have anyone else at tomorrow's meeting besides our department?"* (You already know everyone in your department was invited because of the e-mail list.)

Sally: "Yeah, I asked Ted (the call center boss) and Marie (his assistant vice president) to join us. To get this thing off the ground, we're going to have to attack these small business owners at the call center level."

You: *"I know Ted, but I haven't met Marie yet. Is there anything special I should prepare?"*

Sally: "No, not really. But I am going to try to get our division some bucks from corporate to launch this thing. So any ammo I could get would be helpful. Can you check with the chamber of commerce staff and the economic development people at county and see how many businesses with less than fifty employees there are in our five-county district? Yeah, now that we're talking, I can see that would be great . . . I don't think we've ever put a number to that."

You: *"I can get my hands on that data by the time of the meeting. I know you want to make this happen. What's it going to take for corporate to see things our way?"*

Sally: "Well, it's just about a done deal. I've been doing a lot of behind the scenes work. Now I have to get you guys on board. All I have to do is show corporate I have a good work plan, deliverables from each of you guys, and a reasonable budget, and we'll be set to launch at the beginning of the next quarter."

You: *"What will be the next step after our meeting?"*

Sally: "Well, I'm headed to Chicago in two weeks. If I get the thumbs up, which I'm sure I will, we'll get moving down here and turn some heads in the next year."

Analysis: What a cornucopia of information! You learned that Sally had spent some big-time effort on this, and that she even called in the head of the call center to coordinate the implementation efforts. She's confident this will go. Also, Sally needs some additional information to make her case. You not only helped remind her of these items just by asking the questions, but you are also going to bring the information to the meeting. Finally, you know what's going to happen in the days and weeks ahead. Now you are ready for the second step in preparing for the meeting.

Scenario #2: Handling Production Problems

You chat with the vice president of production every day, so working in your questions about the upcoming meeting will be easy.

You: *"Which way do you think Rich is leaning on this one?"*

Mike: "Well, if my twenty years here have taught me anything, it's that he'll bitch and moan about having to spend more money on a new line, but in the end that's what he'll do because he hates giving money to our competition."

You: *"What do you think?"*

Mike: "I don't mind sending some orders over to Brand X to get through this crunch time, if it means we're going to stop going to the bank to borrow money. We're lucky to have good jobs with a profitable manufacturing company, and I never like seeing us get overextended. But Rich knows more about this stuff than I do. I trust him."

You: *"What can I do to get ready? Does he need any updated production figures?"*

Mike: "No, he has a great handle on that stuff from our weekly production meeting, so you don't have to prepare anything. Just don't try to tell Rich what you think he wants to hear. You'd better be able to prove your point. He hates "yes men," and once he smells that in someone he never takes them seriously again. Of course, don't make the production team look lame by saying something stupid."

You: *"I would never do that."*

Mike: "I know."

Analysis: This little conversation gives you great insight into the meeting. Rich will probably lean toward building a new line, but you can make some points with him by agreeing or disagreeing with him, as long as you make a good, strong argument. You also know that Rich is a good leader and that not only has he refused to be manipulated, but he also has the respect of your boss. This is going to play a large role in your next phase of preparation.

Scenario #3: Winning the Client Back or Letting Go

You're going to go to the head of the department. She's a manager, but not a partner. She's got about five years' seniority on you.

You: *"Robin, is there anything special I should prepare for the meeting with the partners on Friday?"*

Robin: "Yeah, they're going to want to know how the rank and file over at our customer's feel about their new boss. Make some calls over there to your softball buddies and see how much political strength he has."

You: *"Do you think we can do an end run around the new VP?"*

Robin: "Maybe, if we can figure out which way the wind is blowing. Rob (the founder of the firm) may decide to get on the phone with the president of the company and make our case for not getting fired, CEO to CEO."

You: *"Rob would really do that?"*

Robin: "Nobody knows, especially Rob. That's why the meeting is important. We have to decide whether to court the new guy, go around him, or just forget about the business. Rob wanted the partners and the whole department to weigh in. This has become a pretty big deal to him."

You: *"Okay, I'll get on the phone."*

Analysis: Well, this little bit of investigation has led to a new variable: the fact that Rob might take this battle to the mat. The decision making at this meeting has just intensified by a notch or two. Rob might invest a lot of political energy in this issue. You'd better make sure you take your homework assignment seriously.

* * * * * *

Even if you stopped your preparation here, you'd be better off than most of the people who show up at those meetings. You've found out what's on the line, which helps you figure out how to create the strongest connection with everyone in the room when it comes to your time to talk. Also, you've found out in each scenario that there will be something for you to say at the meetings, so you can now move to the next step of the preparation.

Phase II: Preparing Your Input

You've obtained some great inside intelligence about the dynamics of the meetings. You found out what information you can provide to help with the decision-making process. Now take a few quiet moments to put what you learned in the preceding nine chapters to work for you. Start by figuring out what pictures you can paint to make your critical information come alive. You are preparing for the type of performance that can transform you from someone who is considered competent into a colleague who commands the attention of others. This is what the "It" factor is all about.

In Scenario #1 you understand Sally is gung ho on your department taking the lead on this new marketing plan, and that she needs input from all and some data from you to round out her pitch in Chicago. If you support Sally (there's doesn't seem to be any downside, given the facts) you should be thinking about how to make those small-business numbers come alive for Sally and everyone.

In Scenario #2 you know that Rich will probably call upon you at some point during the meeting, and you'd better be able to make your case. There's no political right or wrong with Rich, but he won't stand for a glib yes or no. That means you've got to start figuring out which way you want to vote and prepare a powerful picture to back it up.

In Scenario #3 there's more on the line than you first thought. Rob may want to throw all his weight behind continuing to chase this one client. Your information is one of the critical bits of data Rob needs to make his decision. When it's your time to speak, you'll have everyone's full attention, including Rob's, at least for a minute or two. This is an important moment of communication connection for you. You can spit out how you read the situation as fast as possible, or put some effort into it and enjoy holding the stage for a while longer with your compelling words.

* * * * * *

If you're thinking that this is all a lot of unnecessary work, you're hearing that little voice again. Strong communicators know it's well worthwhile to exert extra effort to understand the complexity of the issues or the political landscape surrounding them. The brief water-cooler conversations and the preparation of your possible input to the meetings give you both the confidence and the necessary information to be able to sit comfortably at the conference table. You now know it's not just a meeting. It's a time to show off your understanding of the company's issues and demonstrate your potent communication skills to Sally, Rich, and Rob. That means the work will have been worth it.

Showtime

The spotlight will turn to you at some point during most meetings you attend, even if you aren't making a presentation. It will come in the form of a request for you to voice your opinion, but don't be fooled. It is showtime when that happens. The others in the room become the audience while you hold the stage. Around the conference table, they will pay attention to you only during your first few sentences before they pass judgment.

If your words command interest, they will mentally stay right there with you, tuned in to your message. If your words are lack-luster, they will drift off, or perhaps even wonder why you are in the room. So your performance at meetings is important to building connections to a number of different colleagues all at once.

That's why you will be ready to launch into your perform-ance, whether you are asked a yes-or-no type question, or a more broad-based question like, "Well, what do you think of our op-tions?" I want to also introduce you to the power of saying, "I don't know, and here are the reasons why." Your goal shouldn't be to have to come up with the right answer to every single ques-tion asked of you in every meeting.

Instead, your goal is to create a connection, so that your words and ideas will add value to the decision-making process. Your prompt for stardom is the expansive rejoinder, " . . . and let me tell you why" or " . . . and let me tell you about that." These words announce to your audience that you have an important opinion or analysis to add.

This is not a time to aim for brevity. It's a time to demon-strate your knowledge and insight. However, here is a single ex-ception to the yes-or-no rule. If the boss of the meeting is taking a quick poll of the attendees on an action item, don't hog the spotlight by using the "Yes, and let me tell you why" tactic. Save it for when the spotlight will rest on you for a minute or two, not during a show-of-hands type exercise.

For example, say that in the financial services meeting Sally turns to you and asks, "Were you able to run down any numbers on how many businesses with fewer than fifty employees there are in our district?" Here then you demonstrate your insight by saying:

"Yes, and let me tell you what I found out from the Chamber of Commerce and the county economic development department. There are over 11,000 businesses in our district with fewer than fifty employees. But the more impressive number is how many employees work in those companies. It's more than a quarter of a million. If we can start doing business with the owners, we stand a much better shot at holding small receptions and small events at their offices, where we can pitch and hopefully sign up a lot of those employees. That's a lot of new customer opportunities for us."

The numbers you used (11,000 and a quarter of a million) take on greater meaning because you've painted a brief picture of what those numbers could mean: receptions and small events where you can sign up new customers. After that little discussion with Sally, your further preparation and your impressive delivery of the information has now created a positive connection with everyone in the room.

In Scenario #2, for a while Rob, the owner, goes round and round with the others at the meeting about the new line and the competition. Then Rob turns to you and says, "You're in the trenches more than any of us. Give us your opinion. What should we do?"

Your answer may not definitive, but it will be insightful:

"I don't know what the best decision is, because I'm not sure how long this sales boom will last. But from a production end, it's going to take at least four months to get the new equipment in here, tweaked, tested, and fully integrated into our systems. That means if we start now, we won't get a lick of relief until well into the second quarter. I've called two different distributors of the type of machinery we're going to need, and they both say the same thing: four months at best. So there's no quick fix here at our plant. Once we pull the trigger, it will be an all-out effort here on the shop floor from both shifts to make the modification to the process that will get the new line up and running. Our guys will have to really sweat to fulfill our current orders and add the new configuration. We won't be able to roll product off that line any earlier than 120 days from now. After that our new capacity will make a huge difference for us."

You have not answered Rob's specific question, but you have made a huge impact on everyone in the room. Your conversation with Mike pushed you to make some calls because you found out Rob wanted hard data. Once you got the facts you fleshed them out with some simple word pictures ("our guys will really have to sweat") that gave your message meaning. This answer is a big communication success for you.

In the third scenario, you've got a big responsibility. Rob needs your information on the political strength of the customer's new VP before deciding how best to move forward. When it comes time for your input, there's no reason not to be forceful:

"Rob, I'd hate to see you waste your energy and your personal equity trying to go around this new VP. The team over there loves him. They say he's fair, full of energy, and already has volunteered to do a lot in the community. He's the type of guy we're going to be seeing around town a lot, so we have to figure out how to win him over or move on and forget about their business. I think you would look unwise trying to pull an end run right now. It could do us way more harm than good."

If Rob is a good leader, he will cherish this information and your strength of delivery, even if it wasn't the news he's been looking for. You've potentially kept the company from failing again and saved Rob from an embarrassing situation. A simple and weak, "Well, it may not be a very good idea, based on what I'm hearing" is not strong enough to win Rob's attention. Instead, your powerful, connective communication shows you've done your homework and can express your ideas fully, even when it's not what others may have been hoping for.

These three meeting scenarios may have nothing in common with your workplace situation or the issues you may face in your conference room meetings. And, of course, you may have to attend scores of purely informational meetings, where you'll never be asked your opinion or to add anything to the conversation. But for every meeting in which there are people with whom you would like to forge a strong connection—bosses, managers, clients, and other coworkers—going through the preparation stages is a critical step. Even if the setting or the politics aren't right for you to say anything during the meeting, your boss might ask you casually, "What did you think of that" as you are both returning to your offices. When you offer well thought-out opinions and dynamic answers that include some detailed word pictures, you will have made a fan. Going through the preparation steps will make you a better communicator in and out of meeting settings. It is standard operating procedure for someone who has "It."

Use the Pause Advantage

Back in Chapter 4 we discussed the importance of pausing before you answer questions with your word pictures. This is critical to your performance in meetings. Your natural inclination will be to pipe up quickly to show you're listening when the president or managing partner asks you to voice your opinion. It's more respectful, more dramatic, and more connective, however, to just pause for a brief moment before you speak. Those who may have tuned out will be brought back in the room as soon as there is a bit of silence. Those who are listening will figuratively move a little closer to hear your words. When you bring a brief stop to the wall-to-wall words that mark so many meetings, you confidently command the attention of everyone. It also gives you that moment to make sure you are painting your picture just the way you want to.

Oh, Yes, There Are Dumb Questions

I encourage you to ask questions in front of everyone. It shows you are in touch with the current discussion and eager to understand the subject. Just stop listening to the "Mommy and Daddy" voice that tells you that there is no such thing as a dumb question, and that your questions will always be precious and delightful to all. Believing that is career suicide. To help you avoid asking dumb questions, here are some quick rules:

• Make sure you are not asking a question to which you can get the answer quickly on your own. If it would only take five keystrokes on Google back at your desk, don't take up everyone's time. To avoid having others roll their eyes and think you're a lightweight, ask for insight, not for easily obtainable facts. In other words, only your Mom would encourage you to ask simple-facts questions.

• Ask your questions with intensity and strength, never with apology:

  • "I am not familiar with the company you mentioned, could you please tell me more about how they might help us?" is much stronger than, "I'm sorry, but I have to ask, what is that company again and what do they do?"

- Use word pictures in your questions, and ask others to use them as well. You can use this tactic to build connections through your questions:

    - "I see our warehouse overflowing and wall-to-wall with products that we should be getting to our customers much faster. Please tell me how you see the new shipping plan alleviating the mess that lies ahead of us?"

- Finally, don't blurt out questions. Be thoughtful, pause, always taking that extra little beat, even in an emotional meeting. If you miss a moment to interject, you'll have another chance later if the matter is important enough.

- Never use a sarcastic question in place of a direct statement:

    - "I can't see us ever increasing sales by hiring reps instead of using our own direct sales team" is much more effective than, "Oh, and I suppose you see these guys who don't even work for us, and who are repping lots of other lines as well as ours, as the missing ingredient to helping spark sales, is that right?"

Remember, only your Mom believes that you can never ask a dumb question. The rest of us will hold you to a higher standard.

After the meeting, following up with the original colleague to whom you directed your questions is a good way to get the most out of the experience. Here are some questions you can follow up with:

- How do you think the meeting went?
- Were my contributions helpful?
- What do you think will happen next?

It's best to ask these questions almost in passing. You don't want to appear needy or insecure, but you do want some feedback. When you ask someone who is trustworthy, they'll be happy to give you an idea of how you did, what mistakes you might have made, and how to avoid them in the future. This is also a nonpolitical and nonmanipulative way of staying in the loop. You're not trying to push your agenda; your goal is simply to be helpful, earnest, and involved. Your follow-up will prove that.

* * * * * *

A meeting is like a performance or an athletic event, and it's the practice and planning ahead of time that leads to success. Once the meeting starts, its game time or show time, and with proper preparation you'll be ready when the spotlight hits you. The action or the agenda you favor may not win, but it won't matter because you'll be heard.

The result for you is that others will take notice, and they may even ask, "What did you eat for breakfast this morning?"—a backhanded compliment that you should enjoy the first time you hear it. It will get even better when they stop by your office later in the day, asking, "What are you doing next Tuesday at ten? We've been talking about it and we'd like your input on the conference call with corporate." You'll smile, knowing they are starting to listen to you.

Observation Assignment

Sit back and observe the flow of ideas during your next meeting (maybe it's later today). When one idea is gaining momentum, try to follow who the champion is and what she is doing to hold everyone's attention. See if you can sense whether she has put some effort into this argument ahead of time, or whether she is just talking off the top of her head.

When someone else in the meeting fails, with his proposal uniformly dismissed after he held the floor for just a minute or two, examine what happened. Try to discern whether it was just a bad concept, or that he hadn't properly prepared how best to discuss his proposal.

Track the flow of energy in the room, and see what's happening when there's excitement and intensity, and when there is a lull or perhaps boredom. In each case try to determine who is responsible.

CHAPTER 11

The "It" Factor Five-Step
Implementation Program

YOU'VE ALREADY TAKEN SOME BOLD STEPS toward your goals of learning the skills that will allow you to create instant and lasting connections—at home, at work, everywhere. You've read through all ten chapters and have, I hope, completed the observation assignments at the end of each one. Each assignment called on you to watch and listen to others. I wanted you to be able to study and contrast the words, the expressions, and the corresponding results of those who have the "It" factor, and those who desperately need it. I specifically designed the observation assignments to be passive.

I wanted you to thoughtfully observe others, taking full measure of the communication tableau, staying distant as possible. Now that you have completed your connection studies you are ready to put the tools to work for you. Let's make "It" a part of your life, starting right now.

I'll introduce a new set of tasks for you for each of the five steps in the "It" Factor Implementation Program. The tasks will require that you use what you've learned in the preceding ten chapters. This means you're going to have to go back and review many of the ideas in order to succeed at each task. Some of the tasks will be a delight to accomplish, others will be a little painful. That's okay. It takes work to get "It."

Some of those tasks will take you several days, others may even take a week or two to complete, and still others you will start and finish on the same day. After I describe each task I'll give you a list of steps to follow to complete the task and show you how to grade your performance. I'm looking forward to your getting straight "A's." Let's go.

Task 1: Cleansing

The Goal

You'll never completely cleanse yourself of the communication sins that are the enemy of the connection-building process. I haven't been able to so, and I know I won't ever succeed in disinfecting myself of them completely. The goal is not to completely eliminate these dastardly words and expressions, but rather to become aware of when and how you use them. Once you build awareness of what is working against you, you will naturally reduce your use of the communication killers. You won't be communication-sin free, but you're going to always be heading in that direction, and that's an important element of the "It" factor. You're going to need some help from others to succeed at this task.

The Assignment

In the days ahead you will concentrate on recognizing *the three communication sins you use most frequently* so that you can drastically cut back their use and eventually eliminate them altogether.

You may not think you use these words very often, but we're going to find out. That's because you're going to pick out three words or expressions that are hurting you, and then you are going to pay people to catch you saying them. Your communication-sin monitors will delight in the exercise and appreciate the few extra bucks you'll hand over. You'll smart a bit and feel a little foolish as you hand over the cash, but you will be on your way to being a better communicator as you become much more aware of your sins.

The Steps

1. Review Chapter 6 and pick out three communication sins you want to work on.

2. Go to the bank and get thirty crisp $1 bills. Roll them up and put a rubber band around them, and put them in your pocket or purse. (If you are on a budget, use quarters. If you've just hit the lottery and want quick results, get twenty $5 bills. The amount doesn't matter, just follow the process.)

3. Enlist the help of two people to whom you are close: one at home and one at work. Tell them the words you want to eliminate and that you want them to be your communication-sin monitors. Promise to pay them a dollar, instantly, every time they catch you using one of the three communication sins.

4. Every time they catch you, pull out the bills and pay them. They will chuckle, you will wince. That means it's working.

Grade Yourself

You'll cough up some money on one sin, more on some others. To get an "A" on this task, you've got to reach that breakthrough moment when you catch yourself just as you're about to use one of your communication sins. Your sin monitor will be disappointed, knowing the gravy train of dollar bills is ending. You will be the one chuckling, knowing the cleansing process is working.

Task 2: Meeting Mastery

The Goal

You should experience being a star, even a minor one, in a meeting. That means walking into important meetings (some regularly scheduled meetings are more information dispersals than an exchange of ideas) with a sense of anticipation, not dread. Yes, meetings can be fulfilling, especially when you are the one being listened to. That's our goal: for you to shine in a meeting.

The Assignment

You will pick a meeting in which you will be able to star. If you have a "change" or "strategy" meeting in the next few days, you'll be able to complete this task in the next week. If you have to wait longer, it doesn't matter. Pick a meeting in which there's a good chance you will be asked to deliver your opinion.

The Steps

1. In Chapter 10, review the steps to becoming a meeting star.

2. Pick your meeting carefully, and prepare well. This is going to be your coming-out party, and I want you to be a hit.

3. Decide whom you will approach to ask your prep questions. Casually get the person alone and fire away:
   a. What is the meeting about?

b. Who will be there?

c. What can I prepare?

d. What do you (they) want to accomplish?

e. What will be the follow-up?

4. Prepare for your role. Decide what you are going to talk about when it's your turn. Do your homework and even go through the meeting scenario a few times in your heart. Picture others nodding their heads in agreement as you speak.

5. It's showtime. Look for your opening and take it. Remember the key prompts for you to shine:

a. "Yes, and let me tell you why . . ."

b. "No, and let me tell you why not."

c. "I don't know, and here's the information I need . . ."

6. Go back to your initial meeting contacts and ask them to evaluate your performance. Ask them for specifics, without appearing needy. You can even say one of your goals is to get better at meetings, so their input is important.

Grade Yourself

If afterward you feel great about the meeting, you get an "A." Your goal is to be a star, and you'll know when you are. A powerful performance will be obvious, even to you. If you followed all the steps and you just feel "okay" about it for whatever reason (it may be politics, over which you have no control), give yourself a "B." Do everything again next week and you'll probably get an "A." If you followed some but not all of the steps, you've failed. You have to go through the whole protocol to succeed. Oh, by the way, you can keep taking this course over until you get an "A." Just keep following the steps until you emerge from a meeting with pats on the back and smiles all around.

Task 3: Time for Your Pitch: Elevator or Ground Floor

The Goal

You've got to "wow" someone you meet for the first time. This can be in an elevator, at a community meeting, or at the kid's gymnastics meet when you are waiting for the awards ceremony to start. You goal is to get them to say something like, "Wow, that's interesting, I'd like to know more about that," or "How did you get started in something like that?" It means your pitch worked and you've connected.

The Assignment

Craft five different elevator pitches and deliver all of them at one time or another in the next few days. This is a lot of work, and there's no way around it. This will also be the task that will be the most rewarding for you, both financially and professionally, so the work will be worth it. You will be needing these five elevator pitches, so there's no reason not to buckle down now.

The Steps

1. In Chapter 7, review the steps for crafting your elevator pitch.

2. Craft your five distinct pitches. You can keep the opening statement the same but use different customer examples and success stories. Write these down if you have to. Your tone should be vibrant and conversational.

3. Deliver the pitches over and over again during the next few days. Don't be picky about to whom you deliver them. Most people like running into others who enjoy their work. Look for positive reactions and requests for follow-up from others. This shouldn't surprise you. You're getting good!

Grade Yourself

This is your toughest task, grade wise. To achieve an "A," you must get the other person to request some type of follow-up: a business card, e-mail, or perhaps a cup of coffee or lunch. You don't have to follow up with them, and you'll find if your pitch is great, lots of people will want to hang out with you more than you want to hang out with them. That's great. You then know what it's like to succeed at making a quick connection. People are giving you their attention and interest. You can pick and choose those you want to follow up with. You don't have to go to the dance, but I want you to get asked. Keep your five pitches going until you get at least one "A." Follow the steps and it won't take that long.

Task 4: Small Talk All Day Long

The Goal

I want small-talk connections to become second nature for you. That means today you will become a small-talk maven. At first you may feel a little uncomfortable as you chat with people you wouldn't ordinarily speak to with any intensity or interest. That's okay. They'll like the attention, and you just might create an instant pleasant connection. It may not bear any professional fruit, but it will make your day brighter.

The Assignment

You must make a meaningful connection with small talk three times today. Note that this is not your elevator pitch exercise. Instead I want you to make a personal connection with someone with whom you would normally only exchange information but rarely have a serious, meaningful conversation.

The Steps

1. In Chapter 9, review the tips to making a speedy connection with small talk.

2. Tomorrow morning, on the way to work, pick a "small-talk friend" and start to make a connection. It can be anybody: the woman making your mocha, the doorman, the guy next to you on the train.

3. At work, pick out someone you know, but don't know very well. Use your small talk protocol with them. This exercise should take no more than three or four minutes. Find out something you didn't know and share something about yourself.

4. After work, pick out another "small-talk friend," just like you did in the morning.

Grade Yourself

In this assignment it's easy to earn an "A." Unless you pick a cretin or someone who is having a miserable day, they will respond with positive vibes to your small talk. After all, your questions will be delivered well and will be flattering to them. Every socially balanced person enjoys having someone else demonstrate sincere interest in them. To get an "A," all you have to do is earn either a "Thanks for asking," or a "Nice talking with you." You will.

Task 5: Compliment and Criticize with Ease

The Goal

Deliver both a heartfelt compliment that will make someone's day, *and* a criticism that will help someone's future performance. This is the easiest of the assignments, which is why we conclude with this one. All you need to be able to successfully compliment and criticize somebody is to follow what you have learned in this book.

The Assignment

Actively look for someone doing something successfully, and tell them about it. Similarly, look for someone who is not succeeding and tell them what they need to do to improve.

The Steps

1. In Chapter 8, review what it takes to make your compliments matter and your criticism helpful.

2. Identify the person to be complimented. Work hard at telling her exactly why you enjoy her success or hard work.

3. Identify the person to be criticized. Make sure you are not apologetic, but instead be helpful as you show him how to improve.

4. Reflect on whether these two people are better or worse off because of your efforts.

Grade Yourself

Follow all the steps and you get an automatic "B." To get an "A," one of two things has to happen. Either you have to witness the complimented person starting to glow, even slightly, because of your words. You'll know it when you see it. Or you can also earn an "A" if the criticized person thanks you for your comments. People rarely compliment others they find bossy or intrusive. When the one being criticized recognizes your connection efforts with a sincere "thank you," you have succeeded.

* * * * * *

Evaluation

Follow all the steps and you'll get all "A's" and "B's." If you get more "B's" than "A's" it may be bad luck, bad timing, or maybe you just have to work harder and focus more. Keep trying. When you earn an "A" for each task of the five tasks, you have demonstrated all the skill of someone who has searched for and earned the "It" factor.

The Delights of Having the "It" Factor

AS YOU HAVE COMPLETED ALL YOUR HOMEWORK and successfully completed the Five-Step "It" Factor Implementation Program, your world is changing in a positive way every day. You are being listened to and you are being understood. That feels great. You are finding that you are also listening to others more, and understanding them better. You are connecting with the guy at the convenience store where you get your coffee, the people in accounts payable at the office, and your neighbor across the street, all in ways you never thought possible. You may find that your disposition is a little sunnier. When you can easily and quickly create connections, the day just has more of a positive beat to it.

And don't be upset when you find yourself backsliding—perhaps popping in a "certainly" or "basically" every now and then, or missing a chance to paint a vivid picture—in a way that hurts your communication efforts. It happens to me every day. I have to be on ever-present guard against making sarcastic remarks, which I know hurt my connections, or giving in to the little voice that tells me I really don't have to work that hard at building new connections. When you have "It," you aren't necessarily perfect in your communication efforts, but you are now aware of what works and what doesn't. That means you're going to connect more often with greater speed than you ever have before. You don't have to be perfect when you are constantly evaluating your communication efforts. Just make adjustments and enjoy the entire process.

The "It" factor is not a peak that you summit. It's a plateau you attain and then hopefully enjoy staying at forever. All the rules, protocols, word pictures, and patience you have now mastered should bring you marked professional and personal success, and perhaps even peace.

Your days will be easier, more relaxed, and will bring you greater pleasure. When communication frustration is significantly reduced—when they are listening to you, liking you, and remembering you—your daily activity becomes more manageable and pleasurable. The work and the patience required to attain "It" will become second nature, but the delight of establishing new connections you never would have made before will always feel new and fresh.

Congratulations. You have the "It" factor, and you will reap the benefits in every conversation, every day.

Index